C000291977

Sermons Preached In The Chapel Of St. Columba's

Charles Hobbes Rice

This scarce antiquarian book is included in our special *Legacy Reprint Series*. In the interest of creating a more extensive selection of rare historical book reprints, we have chosen to reproduce this title even though it may possibly have occasional imperfections such as missing and blurred pages, missing text, poor pictures, markings, dark backgrounds and other reproduction issues beyond our control. Because this work is culturally important, we have made it available as a part of our commitment to protecting, preserving and promoting the world's literature. Thank you for your understanding.

of England and Ireland." It should be added, however, that the Author's opportunities of addressing the boys from the pulpit were so few and of such irregular recurrence, that this is necessarily far from being a complete series of School Sermons.

ARMAGH,
September, 1863.

CONTENTS.

SERMON I.

Weakness and Strength.

[Sunday next before Advent.   November 20, 1859.]

" . . . . . OUT OF WEAKNESS WERE MADE STRONG."
Heb. xi. 34.

THE week on which we have now entered is, to a very large proportion of those now present, the last before their participation in a most solemn ordinance, and their admission to the full privileges of the Christian Church.

Let me now address a few plain practical words to those of you, my brethren, whose Confirmation-day is so very near at hand. And may God in His mercy grant that the words now spoken may help you to spend the few days that remain, before you are presented to the chief pastor of this diocese that he may invoke God's blessing upon you, in cultivating that spirit which He delights to bless.

I have no intention of trying to teach you what the ordinance of Confirmation is. You know that already. Nor shall I try to stir you

B

up to appreciate the importance of approaching this ordinance seriously. If there be—I cannot believe it, but if there be—any one amongst you so hardened as to be making light of it, so foolish as to be blind to the infinite danger of receiving it carelessly; if, even now when it is so close at hand, any one of you be still unmoved at its approach, I cannot hope to influence him by any words of mine. But it cannot be so with you. Doubtless every one of you is really serious about it, really earnest in believing and intending that his Confirmation-day shall be to him the introduction to a godly and a Christian manhood.

But then, what right have you to hope this? Is your intention likely to be carried out? This is the question which I desire to raise in all your hearts, and I will try now to put before you some considerations which may guide you to an answer.

Believe me, it is important to put this question. If you are satisfied with having formed good resolutions, and place your trust in them, it is not difficult to foresee the result. Before long some temptations will come upon you which are different from those which you expected, and for which you had made no preparation; and you will yield to them. And then you will begin to think that you had resolved too much, that you must relax your rules a little. And then you will come to neglect them habitually, and then to forget them altogether. And when, a few years hence, some event happens which brings forcibly before your minds the forgotten vows of your Confirmation-hour—if indeed God be so merciful as to grant you such an undeserved call to repentance—you will be shocked to find how far you have gone astray, too bewildered to know which way to turn, overwhelmed by a sense of the impossibility of recalling those precious years which you will have lost.

It was not by the force of their own good resolutions that they made progress of whom it is stated in the text that "out of weakness" they "were made strong." It is not good resolutions whose triumphs form the subject of that heart-stirring chapter in which these words occur. By faith those great men whose names are recorded there obtained their good report. And it is by "looking unto Jesus" that we are enabled to "run with patience the race that is set before us." The course is the same for us as for them. We have no strength in ourselves; we begin in weakness. But, though in weakness, we are not without hope of becoming stronger. It is true we cannot make ourselves strong; but, if our faith fail not, "out of weakness" we shall be "made strong."

I. The first thing that I would impress upon you, my brethren, is *your own weakness.*

It is hard no doubt to form a fair estimate of this, especially at your age. Bodily weakness is almost unknown to you. You hear old people talk about increasing weakness, but for yourselves you feel that you are putting forth new strength every day, and you cannot realize that you, like all others, are subject to decay and death. And so too with your souls. You have as yet hardly learnt to feel that they are weak and may one day die. It is true, their weakness ought to have been proved to you over and over again. You have failed in temptations which you thought you could resist. But then you have flattered yourselves perhaps that these were trifling matters, that in any great trial it would not be so. And when you have indulged in day-dreams respecting the future, self has always been victorious over the difficulties and dangers which your imagination has conjured up.

Indeed, you would find it hard to believe that you are capable of falling under such temptations as you suppose those to be by which men of maturer years are beset. Good feeling, and the force of those habits in which you are being trained, prevail in you at present, and make you doubt whether it be possible for you ever to sink so low.

And so it would be perhaps if the temptation came upon you now. But how will it be when your good habits have been lost in a whirl of business or pleasure, when the fine edge of feeling has been blunted in the battle of life? Satan suits his weapons to the circumstances of him whom he attacks. If you have not resisted the temptations of boyhood, there is no good reason for expecting that you will by your own strength withstand those which are to come. Look back then, my brethren, as well as forward. While you form good resolutions for the future, trust them only so far as you have found by experience that it is safe to trust them. Let this week be a time, not merely of fervent aspirations, but of close and accurate self-examination. Probe the wounds which you know your foe to have succeeded in inflicting upon you. Be not

store for you. It would be madness to delay
the putting on of your armour *because* the enemy
is getting an advantage over you. In another
year matters would only be worse. No, you
cannot stand in your own strength, you must
seek that which God will give, and you must
seek it in the appointed way. I will not now
do more than just remind you that at this crisis,
when, as I have said, your weakness is greatest,
God offers you, in Confirmation and Holy Communion, new means of grace to strengthen you.

Learn then, as St. Paul learned, to say, "When
I am weak, then am I strong;" "strong," as
last Sunday's epistle taught us, "in the Lord
and in the power of His might." Such strength
may now be yours, if you will seek it in faith.
The opportunity of being confirmed which God
now gives you is a proof that He means this
strength for you. He would dispel your doubts
and fears, as He did those of St. Paul, when he
besought that the trial with which Satan had
been permitted to afflict him might be removed:
"My grace is sufficient for thee: for My strength
is made perfect in weakness." "Seek," then,
"the Lord and His strength: seek His face
evermore." You will not find that He turns

away from you because you are weak. "The Lord"—we sang it in our songs of praise this morning—"is full of compassion and mercy: long-suffering, and of great goodness." "Like as a father pitieth his own children: even so is the Lord merciful unto them that fear Him. For He knoweth whereof we are made: He remembereth that we are but dust."

What if they who, as the Apostle tells us, "triumphed through faith," had not begun in weakness, but had waited to be made strong before they should enter upon their work? What if Moses, "when he was come to years," had chosen "to enjoy the pleasures of sin" and "the treasures in Egypt" "for a season," because he did not think he was strong enough to deliver his people? What if Gideon, and Barak, and Samson, and Jephthah had drawn back when they were called to attack their enemies, because they saw no prospect of success?

We, too, have enemies to attack—those three enemies of our souls which have such terrible power against us—the world, the flesh, and the devil. And we must not sit still, as if we were waiting for God to visit us, to call us on to the battle, and to clothe us with the necessary armour. He has visited us; He has called us; He has placed the armour within our reach. More we must not expect Him to do, till we have bestirred ourselves. We must take to ourselves "the whole armour of God," not wait for Him to force it upon us. We must at once, conscious as we may be of weakness, begin to attack our enemies in faith that God will strengthen us. And then the strength will come. Not all at once: it is a gradual work. We may be hardly conscious of it as it proceeds; for it is not by extraordinary gifts that God helps us; it is by enabling us to triumph over common temptations in the course of our common life. So it is that He encourages us to go on and become bolder and bolder in our ventures for Him. So it is that He leads us on till we trample on those obstacles which once seemed insurmountable; even as Barak, when he triumphed over the mighty Sisera, and sang, "O my soul, thou hast trodden down strength."

We may not hope to do what we should like to do—to make a grand beginning. The gate is strait; the path is narrow. It is hard to find, hard to persevere in it. Its greatest difficulties meet us early on the road. We must expect to be bruised by many a blow, and hindered by many a fall. We must begin in weakness.

But at the end of the course there sits the Judge, holding out to us a crown; cheering us, if we still look to Him in faith, with words of great encouragement, and supporting us as we proceed with fresh supplies of strength. And a great "cloud of witnesses," who have themselves "run the race" before us, stand looking on—patriarchs, and judges, and prophets, and apostles, and martyrs—faithful ones of all ages, from "righteous Abel" down to those last departed ones whom we ourselves have known.

Their eyes are now bent, my brethren, with especial interest upon you. Why should you faint? They once began in weakness, as you are now beginning. What should hinder you from going, as they have gone before you, and as God now invites you to go, "from strength to strength?" Why should not every one of you appear at last, as they have now appeared, "unto the God of gods" in the heavenly Sion?

SERMON II.

The Burden of our Sins.

[Sunday next before Easter. April 1, 1860.]

"ALL WE LIKE SHEEP HAVE GONE ASTRAY; WE HAVE
TURNED EVERY ONE TO HIS OWN WAY; AND THE LORD
HATH LAID ON HIM THE INIQUITY OF US ALL."—
Isa. liii. 6.

THESE words occur in the course of a very
remarkable chapter. Nowhere else in the
Old Testament do we find that any prophet was
blessed with so clear a foresight of the plan of
redemption. We, who are familiar with the
course of events by which that plan was worked
out, are startled, as we read this chapter, to
find how full, how clear a view of them had
been vouchsafed seven hundred years before to
the prophet Isaiah. One after another the in-
cidents on which the Church endeavours to fix
our minds during the present week seem to have
been called up before his eyes. One expression
after another seems to betray an acquaintance, not
merely with the bare outline, but with the minute
details of our Saviour's sufferings.

But the thought which seems to have been predominant in the Prophet's mind is not the manner in which Jesus suffered; it is the object for which He suffered. Over and over again in the course of the chapter he recurs to this, as if it astounded him most of all. It was strange that God should suffer: it was far more strange that He should suffer for man's sin. "He hath borne our griefs, and carried our sorrows;" "He was wounded for our transgressions, He was bruised for our iniquities: the chastisement of our peace was upon Him; and with His stripes we are healed;" "The Lord hath laid on Him the iniquity of us all;" "For the transgression of My people was He stricken;" "Thou shalt make His soul an offering for sin;" "By His knowledge shall My righteous servant justify many; for He shall bear their iniquities;" "He bare the sins of many, and made intercession for the transgressors;"—all these expressions occur in this one short chapter, and prove completely in what light Isaiah viewed the sorrows and the patience, the sufferings and the death of Christ. I desire, my brethren, that we should consider them from the same point of view this morning.

Jesus was, I know, throughout His life, and

more especially in the last few days of His life, our perfect example of patience and humility. The Collect for the day dwells upon this; the Epistle enforces it upon us. And we ought never to be tired of turning our minds to this subject, never to suppose that we see all or nearly all the perfection and the beauty of His bright example. But He was more than this. He was also, when He hung upon the cross, a sacrifice for sin—for our sin—for yours, my brethren—for yours; I say it to each one of you —for yours and mine. And while there is little fear that any of you will fail to be interested in the events of Passion Week, there is great fear that you may forget to associate them in your thoughts with the sins of which you are guilty.

We must not listen to these things as to the tale of some hero's exploits, or some conqueror's prowess. This is not like other records of patient endurance or noble self-sacrifice. We must not simply look on with admiration, as the whole scene passes before us. Let each one of us remember,—It was for me He suffered these sorrows; it was for me He gave Himself a sacrifice; I am the guilty cause of all this suffering.

Do we not all know by experience what it is

to see another suffer for our fault, and in our stead? Which of us has not brought trouble upon a parent, or a brother, or a friend, by his own carelessness, or disobedience, or want of feeling; and has not been overwhelmed with shame when he has discovered the impossibility of undoing the past, or even of helping to bear the burden he has inflicted? Never does the sense of guilt come home to us and overpower us as it does at such times, unless indeed all good feeling is rooted out of our hearts. At no other time do we despise ourselves so much, or hate our sins so bitterly.

Now this is the sort of feeling which ought to work within us during Passion Week. No expression of self-condemnation would seem to us too strong if we could be brought to view this matter in its true light. Thoughts of pride and self-satisfaction would be banished from our minds; and we should be ready, like the woman of Canaan, to bear any name of reproach that might be cast upon us. That comparison of our sinful race to a flock of weak, helpless, senseless sheep—so often used in Holy Scripture, and adopted by our Church in our daily confession of sin—would not seem to us too degrading.

We should not hesitate to acknowledge that "all
we like sheep have gone astray ; we have turned
every man to his own way," if we could be
brought to realize that "the Lord hath laid upon
Him the iniquity of us all."

The season of Lent then is fitly terminated by
this solemn week. Now, if ever,—now, when
we have been engaged in searching our own
hearts, to find out the evil that lurks there unsuspected by others, unsuspected, it may be, till
now by ourselves,—now is the time for dwell-
ing upon the sufferings of Him by whom alone
the punishment of our sins has been borne. Now,
surely, if you have been doing the work of Lent
at all, however imperfectly, you feel your need
of a Saviour. Now, when you are conscious how
disgraceful your actions have been in time past,
and how unpromising your present habits are,
you must feel that, if you are to be saved from
your sins at all, it must be by the help of another,
not by anything that you can do or suffer.

Oh, my brethren, do not let such impressions
pass quite away. Whatever thoughts have been
stirred up within you during the present season,
—whatever sorrow for sin, whatever abhorrence
of sin, whatever desire to be free from the

power of sin,—let the sight of those sufferings which Jesus underwent to save you quicken and strengthen them all.

For it was not with a word that He atoned for them. To sin is easy; to put away sin is a work so great, so difficult, that it was entrusted to no created being but to the Son of God Himself.

In the bosom of the Father there is, and has been from all eternity, a Being co-equal with the Father, "very and eternal God, and of one substance with the Father,"—"the brightness of His glory, and the express image of His person." How great His glory is, how pure His holiness, we know not. We may strain to the utmost all the powers of our mind in the endeavour to realize it, and yet we must fail even to make any approach to it. This great and glorious Being foresaw, before the world was made, all the wickedness that would be perpetrated in it; the acts, and words, and thoughts of vice of which its inhabitants would be guilty; the deeds of cruelty, and treachery, and lust which it would witness; the words of falsehood, and anger, and blasphemy with which it would resound; the fearful profligacy of its great cities, and the

brutish debasement of its savage tribes; the god-
less pride of its enlightened ones, and the slavery
to devils of its ignorant barbarians; the wilful
sins of the ungodly, and the repeated lapses of
the holiest saints; those open acts of wickedness
the recollection of which makes us hang down
our heads for shame, and those secret sins of
which we think so lightly, because as yet no
man has rebuked us for them, no punishment
has overtaken them; all the evil that our strictest
self-examination brings before us, and all that
we have quite forgotten; all the sins for which
each one of us condemns himself, and all those
for which we strive to find excuse. All this He
foresaw; and foreseeing, He pitied the authors of
this evil; and pitying them, all sinful and pol-
luted as they are, He proposed Himself a sacrifice for their sins. And the Father accepted Him
as a sacrifice. The Lord consented to lay upon
Him "the iniquity of us all."

And though He was an only Son, yet it was
with no light, no indulgent hand that God laid
the burden upon Him. Not one jot or one tittle
of the punishment did His Father forego. "It
pleased the Lord to bruise Him." He who is so
kind, so indulgent to us His rebellious children,

who puts our sins away from us "as far as the
east is from the west," exacted all from His
only-begotten Son. There was a moment when
the Son Himself, stedfastly as He had looked
forward and gone forward to that which lay before Him, fainted at the thought of the load
which was just about to be laid upon Him.
Thrice He prayed, in such agony of mind that
a bloody sweat ran down from His body, that
the burden might, if it were possible, pass from
Him. And yet He was obliged to submit to all,
unless indeed He would give up the work which
He had undertaken, and leave our souls to perish.
An angel was sent to give Him strength to bear
it, but bear it He must.

And He did bear it, though all the strength
and all the malignity of the powers of evil were
put forth against Him, though His body was
racked with the sharpest torture that man knew
how to inflict, and His soul was agonized with
all the blackest thoughts that devils can suggest.
He bore it, though those for whom He was bearing it did all that ingratitude, and meanness, and
perfidy could do to make Him weary of the task.
He bore it to the end. Upon the cross He bore
it. After a life during which He had experienced

many of the bitter fruits of sin, He tasted at last
that which is the bitterest of all, the wrath of
God. He became a curse for us. Not like some
faithful martyr to God's truth abiding patiently
his last hour, because he believes that the God
for whom he testifies will stretch forth an unseen
hand to take off any load of sin or weakness
which may be bowing him down, not so did He
encounter death. That hand which has been the
comfort and support of thousands in their last
hour pressed heavily on Him. Then, when He
had known what it was to support the burden,
when not only man but God Himself, His own
Father, had forsaken Him, then He knew that
His work was done. Then at last He laid His
burden down. He cried, "It is finished;" and
His weary soul departed.

What effect, my brethren, shall the comme-
moration of these things have upon our hearts?
Can it be that the story of One who has borne
the burden of our sins for us shall serve to make
us careless and indifferent how much we add to
that burden? "Shall we continue in sin that
grace may abound?" Shall the knowledge that
"Christ has suffered for us, the Just for the unjust, that He might bring us to God," make us

careless about drawing near, or incline us to postpone our approach to Him?

Oh! it was not for this that the glorious Gospel was made known to us. It was that He who was lifted up for us might draw all men unto Him. It was that the love of Christ might constrain us, that we might henceforth live not unto ourselves, but unto Him which died for us and rose again. Can we think lightly of sin when we know how much it cost our Saviour? Can we be content to go on in sin—in any sin—a little longer, because we flatter ourselves that there is time enough to turn, when we know that every sin of ours was laid upon Him?

Yes: nothing is more certain. We can, we do thus ungratefully forget Him. We, the lost sheep, who but for His labour and His love must even now have been wandering hopelessly in the wilderness, we whom the Good Shepherd has sought out and recovered even at the expense of His own life, suffer ourselves to be enticed away from His fold again, and even wait not to be enticed, but wander freely and carelessly to please ourselves. Let us turn then once more to His cross. There is one thought connected with the subject on which we have been speaking which may serve, by God's grace, to lead us back when in our hearts we wander from that cross, and to keep us constant by His side.

In those dark hours of bodily torture and mental anguish, during which the face of God was turned away from Him, and the powers of darkness for a time prevailed, there was a thought of unmixed bitterness which the enemy could insinuate, and doubtless did insinuate, with most triumphant malice.

I mean the thought of those for whom His sufferings would be useless, for whom so much love was being exhibited, so much sorrow borne in vain; of those who, when His death is commemorated in that ordinance which He Himself instituted, invariably, or almost invariably, turn away as though they cared not to dwell upon the subject; of those who are induced by the knowledge that He has borne their punishment only to be careless about adding to their sin; of those who at last, if they go on in their indifference, will, in spite of all He bore, have to bear the eternal punishment of their own sin, because they make no other use of His crucifixion except to crucify Him afresh.

SERMON III.

The Ascension of our Lord a Source of Joy.

[Ascension Day. May 17, 1860.]

"AND THEY WORSHIPPED HIM, AND RETURNED TO JERU-
SALEM WITH GREAT JOY."—*St. Luke* xxiv. 52.

WE see here the effect produced by the
ascension of our Blessed Lord upon those
who witnessed it. Their first impulse was to
worship, their second to rejoice.

Now we can easily understand the first of
these. When we think of the events which
these men had so recently witnessed, the marvels
which accompanied the sufferings and death of
Jesus, the great miracle of His resurrection, and
His appearance to them on various occasions
during the forty days which had elapsed since
that resurrection, in a wonderful manner and
with a glorious form, we feel that they must
have been impressed with a sense of His divine
majesty, they must have been prepared to worship. And then, if we try to realize the scene
witnessed by them on the Mount of Olives; if

we picture to ourselves the earnest conversation, the hands stretched out in blessing, and then the body, that much-loved form, rising silently from the midst of them and passing away into the air, (not, as had happened several times before, vanishing out of their sight so that they knew not whither He was gone, but passing, as they clearly saw, into the heavens,) and then the cloud that "received Him out of their sight," and the two angels telling them whither He was gone, and assuring them that He would one day return; surely, we cannot but allow, it would be a hard, a stubborn heart indeed that would not then instinctively offer Him worship.

But it is not so clear why they should rejoice at this event. The final parting from One who had been so much to them might rather, we should say, have filled them with sorrow. That high privilege of personal intercourse and friendship with Him, which had distinguished them from all other men, was to be enjoyed no longer. His abrupt departure from the earth destroyed at once those hopes of earthly greatness in His kingdom, which had prompted them to ask the question on which He was just conversing with them. And yet they cheerfully obeyed His last command by returning to Jerusalem—obeyed it "with great joy."

My brethren, we shall find, if we look into the subject, that they had good reasons for rejoicing at this marvellous event; reasons which apply to us as much as to them, little as the ascension of our Lord seems to be regarded among Christians now. The celebration of Ascension-day ought to have as much interest for us as that of Christmas or of Easter. Let us see why.

I. The Apostles rejoiced *because He whom they loved was exalted.*

In those days there were some who followed Jesus, as there are some now who bear His name, not because they loved Him, but from other motives. But the Apostles were not among these. They were really His friends. Even in His humiliation they were still attached to Him. It was not love that grew cold on that terrible night when they "all forsook him and fled." In the depth of His abasement some of them proved that they loved Him still. Peter was melted to tears by a look from Him; John was ready at His request to take charge of His bereaved mother.

And now this loved One was exalted. They
saw Him "received up into glory." All doubts
whether they might not have been too hasty in
drawing inferences from His words, whether they
had not exaggerated the meaning of expressions
which had fallen from Him about Himself, and
His followers, and His glory; all fear lest after
all He should prove not to be the Redeemer of
Israel, must have vanished from their minds at
that moment. The mystery was cleared up—
no, not cleared up, but fully accounted for—for
now they knew indeed that He "came from
God and went to God," and felt no wonder that
His words had been mysterious.

We have all known the pleasure of seeing
some one, in whom we take an interest or for
whom we entertain respect, proved by some
strong indisputable testimony to be what we
thought him to be. We rejoice at it for two
reasons; first, because it adds strength to our
own conviction of his excellence, and it is a
great pleasure to us to find that we were not
mistaken; and secondly, because we hope that
it will bring others over to our opinion. We
have all felt this, I say, in some matter great
or small. And our exultation is proportionate

to the value of the test applied, the importance
of the fact ascertained, and our interest in the
person vindicated. Suppose this, then, when the
testimony is the surest, the testimony of God, in
the most important case that can be conceived,
and when the person to whom witness is borne
is one long loved and followed, a constant companion for several years, who has been winning
continually more and more affection, and never
by the smallest act, or word, or look doing anything to forfeit reverence. Such a triumphant
feeling must that of the Apostles have been.

And if we loved Christ, my brethren, we also
should exult because of His ascension, even if
nothing were added thereby to the benefits which
we receive from Him. Do you say that our
knowledge of our Saviour is of a different kind
from that of the Apostles,—that we have not gone
in and out with Him, and become familiar with
the sound of His voice and the sight of His
wonderful works,—that therefore we cannot be
expected to feel so keen an interest in the inci-
dents of His history,—that we must of necessity
be more interested in those whom we see continually than in One whom we have never seen?
You ought not to say so. You ought not to

think so. But if you do, let us take another case.

We know what it is, when we read in history the deeds of great men, or even in fiction those of well-drawn characters, to become identified with those whom we are reading about, to feel a real and hearty satisfaction when we come upon a passage in which their characters are cleared from some false imputation, or they are related to have achieved some great exploit, or to have triumphed over their enemies, or to have made themselves secure in the affections of their friends. We are not deterred by the reflection that, after all, this is not a true story, or if it be true, that the circumstances related are long, long past and have no direct bearing upon us, from feeling a real interest and even a real excitement about them.

Do we feel as much interest in the glorification of Jesus? History tells us of no hero who can be compared with Him. Writers of fiction have conceived no character that has such power to win the sympathies of all mankind as He has. And, besides, He has claims upon our gratitude beyond all other benefactors. Let us then meditate to-day upon His exaltation to the right hand of His Father, till we feel a hearty joy to think that He has received the due reward of His unrivalled achievements, and has had conferred upon Him "a name which is above every name."

II. The Apostles had a second reason for rejoicing when they saw their Lord ascend — in *the benefits which His ascension was to procure for them.*

They knew now, however hard it might have been to believe it when He told them so, that it was expedient for them that He should go away. They knew that two all-powerful Advocates were secured to plead from thenceforth to the end of time on man's behalf, one in heaven and one on earth; One who had ascended to plead for man with God, and One who was soon to descend to plead for God with man.

And we know this, my brethren, yet we feel little joy in the thought of it. This part of our religion is too often forgotten, or slurred over. We find it easier and pleasanter to dwell on that which Christ has done *for* us, than on that which He proposes to do (can I say, which He does? are we suffering Him to do it?) *in* us. It costs us less to acknowledge, to believe in a certain

way, and to rejoice in believing that He has died
to save us from the consequences of our sins,
than to take home to our hearts the truth that
He lives to save us from the sins themselves.
Too often our only fear is fear of punishment,
not fear of sin; fear of God's anger, not fear of
that which makes us subject to it. And thus
the truths of which we are especially reminded
on this day's festival are less appreciated than.
they ought to be.

O my brethren, let us learn to hate our sins
more than we do, and then we shall rejoice, as
the Apostles did, in the recollection of these two
great Advocates who endeavour to save us from
them. Consider what their office is.

The first, our great High Priest, has passed
within the vail, bearing with Him, that He may
offer it to the Father as a propitiation for our
sins, the blood which He Himself has shed. He
is our heavenly Advocate, ever praying at God's
right hand that His all-sufficient sacrifice may be
received on our behalf, ever pleading for each
one of His weakest and most unworthy brethren,
as one after another they fall into sin, that their
sin may be forgiven. " If any man sin, we have
an advocate with the Father, Jesus Christ the

righteous: and He is the propitiation for our sins." And never was there an Advocate better qualified to plead a cause. For He can speak from experience of all that can be said in our behalf; He can plead for us our weakness, or our sorrow, or our sufferings, or our distractions, or the temptations that beset us, for He has felt them Himself. "We have not an High Priest which cannot be touched with the feeling of our infirmities; but was in all points tempted like as we are." It is indeed an inspiriting truth of which this festival assures us. "There is a Man in heaven"—a Man interceding for men at the throne of God; a Man who knows what toil, and danger, and suffering, and anguish, and temptation, and death are; a Man who knows "all our necessities before we ask and our ignorance in asking," and who has pledged Himself to receive and to present before the Father's throne the very feeblest petitions we send up.

The "other Comforter," or Advocate,—for, as you have been often told, the same Greek word is used for both,—does His work not in heaven but on earth, even in the hearts of men. He who went up on high and led captivity captive gave gifts unto men; and the great gift of all was His Holy Spirit, who was henceforth to make Christian men His temple. There was to be no more need for men to cry under the pressure of sin, "O wretched man that I am! who shall deliver me from the body of this death?" For the presence of God the Holy Ghost is, or ought to be, an assurance to every Christian that the reign of sin is over, and that it is possible to "walk not after the flesh, but after the Spirit."

My brethren, do we rejoice at these things? Are we glad to know that a power is given to us which, if we will but trust to it and use it, will keep us safe from sin—that God the Son is praying for us that we may be forgiven for the past, and God the Holy Ghost is present within us to strengthen us for the future? When we are tempted, and feel a wish to do what is right, does the recollection of these great truths come in and make us redouble our efforts? Does it keep us back from a cowardly yielding to the tempter, who would fain persuade us that we are still his slaves? Does it, to borrow the words of Scripture, fill us with "joy in the Holy Ghost?" Is the fruit of the Spirit in us "love, *joy*, peace?"

III. But there is another reason why the ascension of our Lord Jesus Christ is a source of rejoicing to His followers. It is not only a pledge of present grace, it is also *an earnest of future glory.*

The Apostles, just before He ascended, were asking Him about His kingdom. Recent events must have shaken their expectations of an earthly kingdom in whose glories they were to share. As He was parted from them and hidden behind the cloud, those hopes must have received their death-blow. And yet they rejoiced—rejoiced as many Christian men have done, just when all their fondest hopes seemed dashed to the ground, and when their neighbours expected to find them overwhelmed with sorrow; rejoiced, because those lost hopes were replaced by something far higher and more noble, the hope of a heavenly kingdom, the prospect of an eternal triumph. Now they knew that more than they had supposed was meant, when He promised that "in the regeneration, when the Son of Man shall sit in the throne of His glory," they "also shall sit upon twelve thrones, judging the twelve tribes of Israel." Now they saw what was meant by that comforting assurance, "In My Father's house are many mansions: I go to prepare a place for you." Now they knew that heaven

D

and not earth was to be their home, that they
were citizens of another, an unseen country, and
that in good time they should be removed thither
to reign with Him in glory. "This same Jesus
which is taken up from you into heaven shall so
come." This assurance brought them joy.

. And so He deals with us, my brethren. Do
His dealings produce *joy* in our hearts? He
teaches us to set our affections on things above.
In the words of the Collect for this day, He
would have us "in heart and mind ascend" to
heaven with Him now, and hereafter both in
soul and body with Him continually dwell. This
is one great distinctive feature of Christianity.
"Life and immortality" are "brought to light
by the Gospel." It encourages us, not by offers
of worldly success or temporal happiness, but by
a promise, the superiority of which is known to
all who have believed and acted upon it, a promise of life eternal and of heavenly joys.

Most of us are at an age at which it is natural to indulge in visions of future success in this
life, and to cherish hopes of advancement in the
world. Those hopes will never be gratified;
those visions will never be realized. Or if they
are, we shall not find in the reality that happi-

ness which we expected. And the time may come—God send it to us all—when we shall rejoice in the loss of all our worldly hopes, as the Apostles did, in the assurance that we have gained something infinitely better. Theirs is the true joy whose hearts and minds are in heaven, for to them it is a joyful thing to look forward to the only future event of which any of us can be certain, the return of Him who departed on this day.

Do we know this joy? Is the prospect of His return welcome to our thoughts? Let us try to welcome it. We shall never know the secret of true happiness till we have done so. Those whose hearts are set upon worldly objects find the uncertainty of all worldly things a source of constant anxiety to them. But this hope is " an anchor of the soul both sure and stedfast," and " entereth into that within the vail; whither the Forerunner is for us entered, even Jesus." And all who cling to this anchor know that He will see them again, and their heart shall rejoice with a joy which no man taketh from them.

SERMON IV.

Esau and Judas compared.

[Second Sunday in Lent. St. Matthias' Day, Feb. 24, 1861.]

"THE SORROW OF THE WORLD WORKETH DEATH."

2 *Cor.* vii. 10.

IT is not then to be taken for granted that because a man's sins have made him sorry, therefore he is on the way to salvation.   There is indeed
a sorrow which, as St. Paul tells the Corinthians
for their comfort, "worketh repentance to salvation;" and these words have brought conso-
lation to many a broken heart.   But there is
also, and it is very dangerous to lose sight of
the fact, another sort of sorrow which worketh
not salvation but death.   And if we are listening to the call of the present solemn season, and
mourning over our sins, we all need the warning, lest ours prove to be sorrow of the wrong
sort and lead us away from God.

In the following verse the Apostle specifies
the tests by which godly sorrow may be discerned.   It is not my intention now to dwell

on these. The services of this day have, by
an unusual coincidence, brought before our notice the two most signal instances of the sorrow
which " worketh death" which occur in the Bible
history. The first lesson for the second Sunday
in Lent has set before us the vain remorse of
Esau : the festival of St. Matthias reminds us
forcibly of the fall and repentance and death of
Judas. And I trust that, by shewing you one
by one the points of resemblance which are dis-
cernible between these two unhappy men, I may
be enabled to press upon you with double force
the necessity of guarding against that wretched
state of heart and mind in which the only repentance of which men are capable is one which
"worketh death."

I do not forget that the history of Esau suggests many difficult questions. On these I shall
not dwell. Whatever be the correct answer to
them, we may at any rate draw from it that
lesson which St. Paul drew for the benefit of
the Hebrews, and take occasion from Esau's
sad example to enforce that caution which is
so necessary for us all, to "look diligently lest
any man fail of the grace of God;" "lest there
be" amongst us "any fornicator, or profane per-

son, as Esau, who for one morsel of meat sold his
birthright. For ye know how that afterward,
when he would have inherited the blessing, he
was rejected : for he found no place of repentance, though he sought it carefully with tears*."

I. In tracing out the course by which these
men reached their miserable end, the first thing
which strikes us is, that *they had both been re-
markably blessed with religious opportunities.*

Esau had grown up in that family which had
been selected from all others of the human race
to hand down to posterity the knowledge of the
true God; and during his early years he had
been under the influence of the father of the
faithful himself; for it appears that Abraham
lived fifteen years after the birth of Isaac's sons.
Judas had been permitted to join the circle of
those who stood nearest to our Lord, hearing
His words and seeing His works, not on one
occasion only but continually; not, like the
inhabitants of the several villages, when He
came round in His circuit only, but going
round with Him from place to place.

And yet all these privileges could not avail
to save them. Perhaps, for so it has been with

* Heb. xii. 15—17.

thousands, it was an undue confidence in these that worked their ruin. They may have dwelt upon the thought that they were special favourites of heaven, till a fatal security crept over them, till they forgot the necessity of making a right use of those precious opportunities with which God had blessed their souls.

This is a common story. Are there no instances of it amongst us? Men flatter themselves that all must be right with persons who live so much within the reach of religious influences as they do; that, though things may not be taking exactly the turn which might be wished just now, yet they may be sure something will happen to keep them from going very far wrong. Need they be very uneasy who breathe such a religious atmosphere; who pray in private or in public, or receive the Holy Communion, or read their Bibles so much more frequently than others whom they could name?

All the warnings with which God's Word abounds have not sufficed to root out this most deceitful error. It is found even among those who believe themselves most free from it. Guard against it, my brethren, as a subtle device which has been successful in slaying its tens of thou-

sands. Religious privileges are indeed to be
highly valued. They profit, if we will let them
profit. But those privileges slighted or misused
become the very surest weapon in the hand of
the destroyer. They harden the heart more
rapidly and more hopelessly than anything else.
No man falls to so terrible a depth as he who
might have risen to be the very highest.

II. But, secondly, *each of these men had been
called to a sacred office.*

In patriarchal times the firstborn of each family
inherited the office of priest. This was, in fact,
one part of the birthright which passed from
Esau to Jacob. We are not told that Esau was
aware of the prediction uttered by God to Re-
bekah, that "the elder should serve the younger;"
nor, indeed, does it appear certain that this decree
of God would, but for Esau's sin, have involved
the forfeiture of all the rights of the firstborn;
and the history contains hints which go to prove
that Esau regarded himself, and was regarded,
as the hereditary priest of the family[b]. Yet this
is the man whom St. Paul holds up to our abhorrence as a "profane person."

---

[b] Blunt's Undesigned Coincidences, Part I. i. 3.

To Judas, as to the other Apostles, was committed the duty of preaching the kingdom of heaven. In his hands, as in theirs, was placed the power of healing the sick, and even of casting out devils. And yet the devil entered into him, and took undisturbed possession of his soul.

If there be any here who look forward to the sacred office of the Christian ministry, and who are tempted to think that they need not fear the present power of their sins because, when their daily occupation shall be about holy things, such sins must of necessity pass away, let me warn them that the holiest office will not of itself sanctify him who fills it; that even the ministers of God in His Church, like all their brethren in the world outside, find temptations besetting them there. The altar of God is no sanctuary to which our enemy may not approach. Alas! how many who flattered themselves during boyhood that they should somehow or other become good men when they came to be ordained, have lived to find themselves like Esau, thrust out to make room for the more worthy, or like Judas, preaching to others while they themselves were cast away.

The two particulars already mentioned shew that the sad end of Esau and of Judas is one to which all are liable, even those whom men might deem the most likely to be exempt. Their condemnation may be awaiting any of us. Let us, then, be the more careful in tracing the course by which they came to perish.

III. The third point of likeness is *want of faith.* They had no hold upon things unseen. This world was all in all to them.

It is evident, from his contemptuous conduct in the sale of his birthright, that in his heart Esau cared nothing for the promise of a Messiah, who was to spring from the family of his father. Perhaps he would not have distinctly disavowed all belief that that promise had been given or would be fulfilled; but he set no store by it, it was not the foundation of all his hopes. And when he learned, as we read this morning, how his brother had defrauded him, it is evident that it was an apprehension of the loss of worldly pre-eminence, not of spiritual blessing, which extorted from him his exceeding bitter cry.

The first glimpse of the character of Judas which the Evangelists present to us shews a secret disbelief of part of the doctrine of our

Lord. From the concluding verses of the 6th
chapter of St. John it appears that our Lord's
words concerning the necessity of eating His
flesh and drinking His blood had given offence
to many of His disciples, and caused them to
withdraw from His company. He asks the twelve,
"Will ye also go away?" Peter indeed pro-
fesses faith on behalf of his companions; but
his Master, who read their hearts, made then
His first allusion to the traitor who was among
them,—"Have I not chosen you twelve, and one
of you is a devil?" And we are taught to con-
nect the fall of Judas with the failure of his faith
at this time. For the present there was no per-
ceptible difference; he seemed to be a believer
still. A year or two later, on the very night of
the betrayal, the eleven, who had been his constant companions all the time, had no suspicions
to guide them when they were taxed with having
a traitor among them. And yet faith was then
so completely extinguished within him that, when
shame did at last overcome him, his only feeling
was that he could not face the world; he hastened
to that place where, if the least spark of faith
had been alive in his heart, he would have known
that everlasting shame awaited him. And yet

up to the very last night this man passed for
a faithful and attached disciple.

In the same manner we cannot doubt that
men thought well of Esau, as even Isaac appears
to have done. And indeed such a character is
generally popular. It is, we are told, no great
harm if the wild spirits of the young lead them
to treat religion somewhat carelessly, as he did.
He had a good heart, perhaps they thought; for
men accept that generosity, in which he certainly
excelled, as an evidence of more than it really
proves. Good feeling is not faith; generosity is
not faith. We ought never to trust men when
they assign to us good qualities which we suspect
not to be really ours. We ought not to be satisfied
with any good habit, however fair a show it may
make, which is not founded upon a stedfast faith
in God and in His Word. Men cannot tell which
of their neighbours are rooted and grounded in
faith. We know it of ourselves. We can ascertain whether the strength by which we resist
the power of any class of sins is a strength which
comes to us from on high in answer to the prayer
of faith, or whether it is merely the strength of
our own will, which is able, no doubt, to hold us
back from those sins to which the ruling passion

does not happen to incline us, but which can never expel sin altogether from the stronghold which it establishes within us.

IV. For, to pass on to a fourth point, those whose conduct is not founded upon faith are sure, before long, to fall under *the dominion of some besetting sin.*

In Esau, sensual indulgence, in Judas, the love of money, grew like thorns among the good seed, till they had gained the mastery; till at length the one could barter away his birthright with a jest to satisfy his appetite, and the other could propose to sell his once beloved Master for thirty pieces of silver.

And it is so with all who do not walk by faith. The goodliest promise fades away; the worst presentiments are realized. The test is not freedom from some particular class of sins, but freedom from the dominion of any sin whatever. It is easy enough to pick up armour which will protect us at this point or at that from the fiery darts of the wicked one. At one place good and generous feeling is sufficient; at another, refined tastes will keep us safe; at a third, ambition; at a fourth, the love of parents or friends. But it is vain to attempt to keep off evil altogether

while we depend upon such safeguards. Nothing
but the "shield of faith" will do for all occasions
and for all forms of attack. Without this we
may beat off Satan here or there; but he will find
out our weak point; he will find a way to wound
us somewhere.

We may feel the wound and think little of it,
confident that upon the whole we are doing well.
And so we may go on, till it is too late to doubt
its dangerous nature, and, oh! perhaps also too
late to apply the certain cure.

So it was with Esau and with Judas. But I
must reserve the sequel for another day. Enough
has now been said to shew you how they came
to that condition in which repentance was impossible. Neither of them had meant to go so
far; neither of them supposed that he was going
so far. Let me, in conclusion, entreat you to
make strict enquiry of your own hearts whether
you are travelling along the same path. Have
you begun to presume upon your privileges, to
feel too certain that you are safe? Have you
lost by degrees the clearness of that eye of
faith to which things of the unseen world become evident and sure? Have you then become, unconsciously perhaps, the slave of some

sin which you thought you were only indulging very slightly for a time?

If you find this to be the case, be sure of this—that upon the road along which you are proceeding there is a step—you know not, I know not, how near to the place where you now stand—beyond which if you once pass there can be no return. You may reach it, without knowing where it is; you may pass it, unconscious how far you have gone. You can draw back now, but then the powers of hell will hold you fast. If sorrow for sin take no hold upon your hearts until you have passed that step, sorrow itself will only work your death.

Therefore, my beloved brethren, "take heed lest there be in any of you an evil heart of unbelief," tempting you to "depart from the living God," and leading you half unconscious among the paths of sin. Draw back now while you have opportunity, and while He is ready to receive you. "Return unto the Lord" now, "and He will have mercy, and to our God, for He will abundantly pardon."

And if your hearts are telling you that there is a very good reason why you should not begin your return to-day, remember that "He limiteth a certain day." I cannot tell you how close at hand that limit may be. I cannot promise you that, if you delay till to-morrow, you shall not find that the time is past; that you are buffeting with the waves of that great water-flood, out of which no man ever escapes to come nigh Him.

SERMON V.

Esau and Judas compared.

[Third Sunday in Lent. March 3, 1861.]

"THE SORROW OF THE WORLD WORKETH DEATH."

2 *Cor.* vii. 10.

YOU may remember that I brought under your notice last Sunday the history of two men to whom the services of the day had directed our attention, and in whom we find the most remarkable instances of that sorrow which is spoken of in the text. I pointed out to you that Esau and Judas fell into that abyss which is beyond the reach of repentance in spite of very high privileges with which they had been blessed, in spite also of the holy calling with which they had been called. And I told you of the hints with which Holy Scripture supplies us that we may trace the course of their fall: how, first, it is evident that they lost that firm hold upon God and the things of God which faith alone could give, and became simply men of this world; and how want of faith led them, as it leads all, into

E

positive transgression; and how they became enslaved, each by his own besetting sin.

Thus far it is no difficult matter for any one,
who by God's grace is so disposed, to consider
whether he may not himself be affording another
instance of the same unhappy course. It is
a common one. Indeed, it is in some measure
within the experience of us all, for there is no
man who has not at some time let go his faith
and fallen into sin. Some, by God's grace, are
recovered from so dangerous a state. But who
can tell how many go on too long, go on till
they afford a parallel to those two whose lives
we are considering, in the end of their course
also? Need we go out of this chapel to find
cases where the danger of such a persistence in
evil is imminent? God knows.

At any rate, my brethren, let me try to fix
your eyes upon those two beacon-lights which
God's Word holds up to warn you off the dangerous ground. Let me shew you how the parallel
which we began last Sunday may be continued.
I cannot appeal to experience in confirmation of
what I have now to say. Holy Scripture has
lifted up the veil, and has distinctly told us what
was the end of these men. The fate of others

remains still a secret, and must remain so till the last judgment shall reveal it. Thank God, our hope is not yet quite extinguished. But we may be assured that the end of the reprobate is most certainly before us, if we persist in living as Esau and Judas lived. Every step we take along the path of sin will be harder to retrace than the last. And there is, as I said last Sunday, a point at which the difficulty of return becomes actually insurmountable, a step after which we shall find no place of repentance.

Yes: but then, your sinful heart suggests, we are a long way from such danger as that. We are but young, and men who have grown old in sin have ere this been recalled from the paths of death. Now this is just the state of mind which is most dangerous. The indulgence of such a feeling as this carries us on of itself a long way towards the fatal spot. Some men reach it, we must fear, much earlier in life than others. No one is so likely to be near it as he who is confident that he need be under no alarm.

V. The next point of resemblance between Esau and Judas is this evident *unconsciousness that the critical moment of their life was at hand.*

They seem to have had at the time no idea of
the enormity of the guilt which they were in-
curring. Both were startled when they discovered how far their sin had carried them.

And it is always so, my brethren. God does
not hold us back forcibly from ruin. We do
not, therefore, see the end of our course from the
beginning. Temptations come upon us gradually,
in such a form as Satan thinks most likely to
deceive and ensnare us; and it is not till we
have yielded that we know distinctly what we
have done. The step which lies before us seems
easy and natural; a step further on the way to
death no doubt, but not involving any immediate danger, and one which we can easily retrace. So it seems till we have passed it. Then,
if we look back, we see what wide leaps we have
been taking, how steep the ascent would be if
we tried to go back, how much we should have
saved ourselves if we had desisted a little while
ago. You know that this is always the case.
Do not then dare to deceive yourself by the
thought that you do not see the approach of any
great crisis. Satan may, for all that, be preparing you to take some fatal step. He may be
beguiling you into a state in which his very

worst suggestions will not shock you. It may be he has found out your besetting sin, and plied you with temptations; first to think about it, and then to commit it in some slight and, as you thought, trifling form; and then to repeat it; and then to go on to worse forms of it; and at last to become quite a slave to it; rendering you familiar with its grossness by such slow degrees, that you have at no time been startled at the progress you were making in his service.

Thus it is that he leads on the sensualist, who like Esau is becoming a pitiable slave to the lusts of the flesh, unable to resist the least of their promptings, even when the indulgence has ceased to give him pleasure. And thus too that he blinds the eyes of those who like Judas are serving mammon. Thus it is that he is carrying away securely the souls of thousands, who trusted that their own wisdom would suffice to warn them when it was time to draw back, and their own strength would be strong enough to take them back; and who would not see the necessity of a constant exercise of faith in God, and of a constant watchfulness against every temptation to wilful sin.

VI. Another thing observable in both these

men is, that at the time when they placed themselves beyond the limits of God's mercy they
were both men *with a great deal of good about
them.*

Indeed, Esau's history seems designed almost
to teach us this lesson, that, though all may be
well in every respect but one, one failure wilfully allowed destroys the virtue of the rest.
The sin of Judas is one far less popular than
Esau's, and one for which we find it harder to
make allowances. Yet even he shews evident
signs of good. His repentance, such as it was,
went a great way. He confessed his sin, and
he declined to keep the money he had earned,
when he realized what his bargain involved.
And confession and restitution are among the
most hopeful signs of true repentance. Yet he
was not, and was incapable of becoming, truly
penitent.

What madness then must it be to go on trust-
ing in the good feeling which is sometimes
stirred up within us, or the exertions after good
in some form which, now and then, we are disposed to make. These things are compatible
even with the hopeless condition of the reprobate. They can therefore afford no proof that

we are not hastening towards reprobation. The hateful character which is stamped indelibly upon the reprobate man is never fully discerned in this world. It would be a great mistake in the policy of our enemy if he urged men on (however firmly he might hold them in his grasp) to exhibit themselves in all the foulness with which sin is investing them. The sight would be so horrible that it would raise the alarms of others whose destruction he has well-nigh compassed. Seldom therefore, if ever, can one man see that another is given over to perdition.

And indeed our business is not with others. Let each for himself take warning that Satan does not all at once make his victims hateful to themselves. It is by the deceitfulness of sin that men are hardened. What gain is it to the man who is doomed to die for murder, that he never broke the laws against any other crime? what comfort to him on whom fever has laid its deadly hand, that his constitution is quite sound? One crime makes a man amenable to the laws; one disease is sufficient to kill the body: one sin can plunge our souls into hell.

VII. There is one more point yet to be noted.

How can it be said that a man is given over
hopelessly to destruction while he yet lives?
Does the grace of God fail? Is the offer of salvation not extensive enough? If Esau and Judas
had repented, and had returned to grasp the
hope which God holds out, would they not have
been received? No doubt they would. But
mark the truth to which this subject tends—*they
could not return.*

The danger is not because God hesitates to
receive those who are late in seeking Him, but
because delay makes it difficult, and at last impossible, for men to set about seeking Him. It
is because the sorrow which the reprobate feel
is remorse and not repentance. Godly sorrow is
out of their reach. God the Holy Ghost, who
alone can infuse it into men's hearts, has deserted them, and will strive no longer with
their sin.

Can you find in Esau's bitter grief for the
punishment of his sin one single symptom of repentance for the sin of profanity itself? Do you
see in Judas any sign that his heart was being
drawn towards God?

The undoubted tendency of sin is this, to lead
men on more and more blindly towards the

darkness of damnation, to deprive them of the power of sight which they have long ceased to use; so that at last, when the darkness has become so gross that it may and must be felt, they may turn, but their sightless eyes discern none of those bright beams of light which are ever emanating from the countenance of God.

Such, then, may be the end of a life which is begun with every hopeful sign. These men of whom we have been speaking were not monsters of iniquity, but men like ourselves. They had been brought within the reach of influences as promising as any that we have known. And yet they came to this; and it is possible for us to follow them.

Oh! that I could induce those of you who know that there is in them any "root of bitterness" to "look diligently," lest they "fail of the grace of God." May He enable us all to root out from our hearts not one alone but all of those fleshly lusts which ruined Esau, and of those worldly lusts by which Judas was destroyed. May He take away from us all vain presumptuous confidence, and lead us on to honest earnest efforts after holiness. Then we shall never be beguiled into the thought that we may safely suffer ourselves to be carried away by temptation for the present; then we shall not abuse His long-suffering by delaying because to-day is too soon to return, but shall seek Him at once with fear and trembling, lest to-morrow should prove too late.

SERMON VI.

The Third Psalm.

[Third Sunday after Easter. April 21, 1861.]

'I LAID ME DOWN AND SLEPT, AND ROSE UP AGAIN: FOR THE LORD SUSTAINED ME.''—*Ps.* iii. 5.

IN following the history of David,—the man about whom more is told us in the Bible than about any other man, excepting only Him who is God as well as Man,—our daily course of lessons has brought us during the past week to the saddest period of his life. On Friday we read* how, just when he had reached the very acme of worldly prosperity,—when the house of Saul had been completely vanquished and all Israel acknowledged him cheerfully as king,— when all the neighbouring tribes, the Philistines and the Syrians and the Edomites and the Moab-ites, were subdued, all except Ammon, and the war against Ammon was just on the point of ter-minating successfully,—just when he was as pros-perous as he could possibly be, he fell into that

* 2 Sam. xi.

grievous sin which casts so dark a shadow upon his character. We read also how, as usual, one sin led to another, and how he continued for many months impenitent and hardened.

Yesterday we were told in the morning [b] how at last God by the prophet Nathan sought him out in mercy, and brought him back to that state of sorrow and repentance, from which it seems so strange, so unaccountable (to all who have not known and felt how subtle and how strong sin is) that such a man as he could have kept himself back so long. We heard too how, though his sin was forgiven, its chastisement could not be foregone; and how division and distress in his family were denounced against him as a righteous retribution to be exacted throughout the remainder of his life. The evening lesson [c] told us something about the fulfilment of that threat. And the chapters [d] for which the Sunday lessons have been substituted to-day, and those which will be read to-morrow, carry on the melancholy story. They tell us of that which was the bitterest drop in David's cup of sorrow, the conduct of his favourite Absalom; who, after a long estrangement followed by kindness and forgiveness on his

[b] 2 Sam. xii.   [c] Ibid. xiii.   [d] Ibid. xiv.—xvii.

father's part, endeavoured to supplant him in the affections of the people, and being at length successful broke out into open rebellion.

We read there how the news was brought to David that he was no longer (what he had been all his life) the favourite of the people; that he must realize the fact of his being an unpopular man; that "the hearts of the men of Israel are after Absalom [e]:" how he and his household were constrained to seek safety in immediate flight, to leave home behind them, to turn away from Mount Sion where stood the tabernacle in which he loved to seek God's presence; how that mournful procession of the few who still remained faithful "wept with a loud voice" as the King "passed over the brook Kidron," and turned "toward the way of the wilderness," and "went up by the ascent of Mount Olivet, and wept as he went up, and had his head covered, and went barefoot: and all the people that was with him covered every man his head, and they went up, weeping as they went up [f]."

We read [g] how he was told that Ahithophel, the counsellor in whom he had placed most confidence, had turned traitor; how the King was

---

[e] 2 Sam. xv. 13.   [f] Ibid. xv. 23, 30.   [g] Ibid. xv. 31.

constrained to accept provisions from Ziba, a mere
servant of that house of Saul over which he supposed himself to have triumphed for ever[h]; and
how, as he went on, a member of that house
came out and cursed him and cast stones at him
with impunity[i].

That was a night of sadness for David; but
his God had not quite forsaken him.

The psalm from which my text is taken, and
which, as the title informs us, refers to that
night, tells us how he felt and how he was enabled to bear the sorrows which God had brought
upon him.

He was not insensible of them. David was
not the man to be callous at the loss of friends
or relations. He felt, and felt acutely, more
acutely because of that sting of self-reproach
which told him that they had some right to regard him as one on whom God was taking ven-
geance. We are not surprised then to find that,
at this time, as he heard how one after another
of those on whom he relied had turned away, he
burst forth into the passionate cry, "Lord, how
are they increased that trouble me: many are
they that rise against me. Many one there be

that say of my soul: There is no help for him in his God."

But, stricken and afflicted as he was, he knew that God's anger would last only for a time; that he was not given over for ever into the hands of his enemies. There was comfort for him still. He could not, indeed, as he was accustomed in his troubles, seek out the holy hill where the tabernacle stood; but he could and did pour out his prayers to the God who dwelt there even from the wilderness. And those prayers were heard. "But Thou, O Lord, art my defender: Thou art my worship, and the lifter up of my head. I did call upon the Lord with my voice: and He heard me out of His holy hill."

Ahithophel had begged Absalom to let him pursue David that night and smite him while he was weary[k]. Hushai, who was in David's interest, but had affected to go over to Absalom in order to defeat Ahithophel's counsel, induced them to wait till morning. Meanwhile he had his trusty messengers, the sons of Zadok and Abiathar the priests, by means of whom he was enabled to make David acquainted with the enemy's plans, and to advise him to push across

[k] 2 Sam. xvii. 1—22.

the Jordan that same night. And so that night did not witness his destruction. "I laid me down and slept, and rose up again: for the Lord sustained me."

And having been thus delivered, he could cherish the hope that a more complete deliverance was in store for him; that the contest would terminate in his favour, however great the multitude who had now turned against him. "I will not be afraid for ten thousands of the people: that have set themselves against me round about." He could feel persuaded that those ten thousands, who were hot upon him, like the ravening beasts of that wilderness in which he was sojourning, would be disabled from devouring. "Up, Lord, and help me, O my God: for Thou smitest all mine enemies upon the cheek-bone; Thou hast broken the teeth of the ungodly." He could commit the cause of himself and of his people to One who had already proved His willingness to bless. "Salvation belongeth unto the Lord: and Thy blessing is upon Thy people."

Thus much concerning the original meaning of this Psalm. And if it bore no other application, its beauty would be well worth our observation, and its instructive lessons manifold and forcible.

I will not now stop to point out in detail what these are. But one remark I must make.

The circumstances of the author were such as are at present perhaps unknown to most of us. A night of danger and anxiety, caused by the loss of friends or by unnatural conduct on the part of those whom we loved best, is a thing which few of us have ever experienced. And our morning thanksgivings are too often offered coldly, if they are offered at all; our sense of the readiness of our heavenly Father to comfort and to save us is feeble at the best. And it may be we shall not all be called to bear that same trial which was the lot of David; it may be we shall never find ourselves hated by those men who used to love us, and attacked by those who once looked up to us with reverence or admiration. Yet in one respect all are like David. The time will come when we shall feel the hand of God laid heavily upon us in some way or other, and we shall know that He is exacting a just retribution for our sins. And though we may not find men assuming that God hates us and is giving us over to destruction, yet we shall hear the subtle voice of many devils plying our hearts with false temptations to despair, and saying,

F

"There is no help for thee in thy God." And we shall be half inclined to believe that the weight of sin which we feel to be pressing us down is beyond all hope of remedy; that all our efforts to remove it are vain and profitless; that it is useless to try to repent, because God's face is turned away from us.

Oh! believe it not. They are no true sons whom their Father chasteneth not when they require chastisement. He is purging away your sins : He is not willing for you to perish. Call upon Him with your voice; and He will hear you out of His holy hill. Seek Him, like David, even when His presence seems to be most angrily withheld. To borrow the language of other Psalms written at the same period, "like the hart that thirsts for the waterbrooks [1]," or like the wanderer "in a barren and dry land where no water is [m]," even so desire more and more earnestly the dew of His blessing. It will not be withheld for ever. In His own good time He will bless you with a sense of security, which shall enable you, like David, to trust in Him that He will save you from the enemies both of your soul and of your body, to commit yourself

---

[1] Ps. xlii. 1.   [m] Ibid. lxiii. 2.

in full assurance to His care; to say in the evening, when you are weary and alarmed, " I will lay me down in peace, and take my rest : for it is Thou, Lord, only that makest me dwell in safety [n] ;" and in the morning, grateful for safety and refreshment, " I laid me down and slept, and rose up again : for the Lord sustained me."

But these words have another and a higher application, which we must hasten on to make. That night of sadness in David's life reminds us of another sadder night in the life of David's son. That valley through which the Kidron flows, those slopes of the mount of Olives, have been the scene of sufferings more intense, of an agony of more thrilling interest, than those of David and his friends. There David learned the treachery of Ahithophel; and there Jesus felt the treachery of His familiar friend whom He had trusted. There those sufferings began in which He was to experience what it was to be left, not as David was with a few faithful adherents, but quite alone; to be deserted, out of cowardice, even by those who really loved Him. There the three with whom He was most intimate fell fast asleep within sight of His in-

[n] Ps. iv. 9.

tense agony; there the eleven who had continued faithful hitherto "forsook Him" at the
sight of His enemies, "and fled."

And then the weary hours of that night passed
away; and morning made it known to the whole
city that He was on his trial, and brought crowds,
who but a few days before had led Him in triumph
through the streets, to clamour for His death.
How do these words of David seem as if they
had been written for Him, "Lord, how are they
increased that trouble me: many are they that
rise against me."

And then He hung upon the cross, and heard
the mocking words of men who ought to have
been the guides and leaders of their brethren
unto truth: "He saved others; Himself He cannot save;" "He trusted in God: let Him deliver
Him now, if He will have Him." Many there
were indeed that said of His soul, "There is
no help for Him in His God."

Yet He knew that God was His defender, His
worship, and the lifter up of His head; and He
did call upon the Lord with His voice, and He
heard Him out of His holy hill. "When He
had offered up prayers and supplications with
strong crying and tears unto Him that was able

to save Him from death," He "was heard in that He feared." For a time, indeed, the dark cloud of our sins in which He was enveloped hid from Him even the light of His Father's countenance, but only to make Him the more earnest in His prayers until they were answered. And the agonized cry, "My God, My God, why hast Thou forsaken Me?" was exchanged for, "Father, into Thy hands I commend My spirit." And so He laid Him down in peace, and slept the sleep of death. "And rose up again, for the Lord sustained" Him.

That night was no more fatal to Him, as His enemies had vainly hoped it would be, than the night on which David fled had been to David. And having risen again, He sounds the note of Easter joy and confidence for us His followers. He does not withdraw Himself from us, but is with us still; with us whom He has called to die with Him, to die to sin and to rise again unto righteousness; with each one of us, as the Captain of our salvation, guiding, instructing, encouraging. Into our mouth, then, as one who is united to us, He puts the cry, "I will not be afraid for ten thousands" of evil angels, "who have set themselves against Me round about."

He encourages us to pray, "Up, Lord, and help
me, O my God." He bids us believe that " salvation belongeth unto the Lord," and that His
blessing is upon all His people.

And if we will intrust ourselves to Him, in
full confidence that He will guard and guide
us in that contest with sin in which He Himself
has fought and won, then no prospect of danger
need alarm us. The shades of night—that dark
night of death which lies between each one of us
and the morning of eternal safety—will not ter-
rify; for we shall know that He is with us, His
rod and staff will comfort us in our passage
through the darkest of valleys. And on the
morning of the resurrection our note of praise
shall blend with the voices of ten thousand times
ten thousand whom, like ourselves, He will have
enabled to triumph; not, as we raise it now too
often, carelessly or coldly, but from hearts over-
flowing with gratitude,—"I laid me down and
slept, and rose up again: for the Lord sustained me."

My brethren, these things are not an idle
dream. They are solemn, and they are real.
Do not put away the thought of them, as if
they did not concern each one of you. Learn,

while you have time, from the example of David how to suffer, and much more intently at the cross of Jesus how to die.

Suffering and death are among the penalties which God has attached to sin, and not one of our sinful race can escape them. But we may meet them in such a spirit as to change our curse into a blessing. Let us learn from the Psalm now before us what that spirit is.

It is the spirit of perfect faith in God our Saviour, and perfect resignation to His will. The heading of the Psalm tells us that its subject is "the security of God's protection." There is no other source of security which never disappoints. For all of us, whatever be our lot, in darkness or in light, in suffering or in joy, in life or in death, there is but one unfailing ground of confidence, — "The Lord sustaineth me."

Why then are we so little inclined to trust in Him—so careful, so eager, so anxious about sustaining ourselves? The strong man trusts to his strength, the influential man to his power, the rich man to his money, the clever man to his policy : and all, one after another, are destined to be disappointed. Let us, my brethren, commit our cause to our Father which is in heaven; let us trust that, however heavily His hand may press upon us at times, the weight will be removed in due season. We shall not suffer one day longer than it is good for us to suffer, if only we will let suffering work its work upon us. He gives us proof from time to time, while the enemy is upon us, that He hears us out of His holy hill, that He is our defender and the lifter up of our heads. And when the necessary discipline has been fulfilled,—discipline which He has no pleasure in prolonging, but which our frailties render necessary,—then all enemies, even the last, shall be destroyed; and His blessing shall descend in all its fulness upon the people who have patiently waited for His coming.

SERMON VII.

Prayer and its Impediments.

[Twenty-second Sunday after Trinity. Oct. 27, 1861.]

"LORD, TEACH US TO PRAY."—*St. Luke* xi. 1.

NO doubt you all remember what reply our Lord made to this request. Only two days ago we read how it induced Him to repeat that form of prayer with which He had before instructed His disciples to approach the Throne of Grace, which is familiar to the very youngest of us by the name of Him who taught it—the Lord's Prayer. And how could a more useful or a more complete lesson upon prayer have been given to the enquirer?

It is not, however, about our Lord's reply that I am going to speak to-day. If it please God to bless what is now said, you will for yourselves turn to that prayer, and learn its holy lessons with more attention perhaps than you have ever given to it before. My wish is to stir up thoughts in the heart of each of you, my brethren, which

may convince him of the necessity of seeking
Divine assistance in the task, and dispose him to
apply to Jesus with the same request which one
of His disciples made in the text,—"Lord, teach
me to pray."

I will tell you plainly why I have chosen this
subject. It is of course a very important one at
all times, and never out of place in a sermon to
Christian people. But there is a special reason
for bringing it forward here. There is no place
in the world where the neglect of prayer is more
dangerous than it is here. There is no family,
no household, no body of persons living together,
where it is more certain that the enemy of our
souls is trying to drive away thoughts and habits
of prayer than here amongst us. There is no
congregation where he is a more regular attend-
ant than here in this chapel. Is there any one
of us who could say with truth that he has never
welcomed him? Oh! how often have we offered
him a place in our hearts, and found that he does
not wait for a second invitation!

It is a solemn thing, believe me, for those
who are intrusted with your souls, to look round
upon the congregation which assembles daily in
this place, to think of the opportunities of learn-

ing to pray which are here bestowed upon you, and of the ease with which you can, if you please, turn them into a curse.

The Church to which we belong bids us teach you, that you are not able to do those things which God commands " without His special grace, which you must learn at all times to call for by diligent prayer." Do you believe us when we say so? Do you in your hearts distrust yourselves and your own strength, and feel the necessity of leaning upon God for support? We can press the lesson upon your attention, but we cannot force it into your hearts. It must be left to you to accept or to reject it, as you will.

The College, too, which has received you here lays its solemn charge upon us. It bids us call you together daily for public prayers, and bids us also take care that ample opportunity is afforded to each of you for private prayer.

God only knows what fruit this holy care for you has produced, or is producing. But this we know, that they who will not gain by it must of necessity lose more than they suppose; that they who leave this place without the spirit of prayer infused into them must be in tremendous peril. None enter upon manhood at so great a disadvantage as those on whose earlier years much care has been expended in vain.

You may doubt this perhaps. You may suppose that it will be easy enough for you to pray, whenever you want to pray. And so you may go on neglecting opportunities, despising admonitions, hardening yourselves in godlessness. But, whether you believe it or not, the fact is sure. And you will believe, you will know it, hereafter.

Let me offer you to-day a few plain and simple remarks about prayer, in the hope that you may be induced to guard in time against the growth of prayerless habits, and thus to save yourselves from much unhappiness in days to come.

I say I want to make some plain and simple remarks. I am not going to talk cant to you. Nothing is more dangerous, when we are upon such subjects, than to fall into a way of using expressions which we do not quite feel or understand, simply because we hear other people use them, or we find them used in religious books, or we think they express what we ought to feel. Let us be natural and unaffected about this matter. Do you, my brethren, know by experience what it is to pray?

To avoid confusion and (what is likely to follow if we are confused) self-deceit, let us now try to answer in order the following simple questions:—What is prayer? Why is it necessary to pray? What hinders us from praying?

I. What is prayer?

Need I tell you that it is not the mere bowing down of the body, or clasping of the hands, or the repetition of certain words with the lips? You all know that the heart and mind must be engaged in the task, or there is no true prayer. But there is still room for mistake. Mind and heart may be engaged, and yet we may not be praying.

Thinking good and holy thoughts is not praying. We might go through the whole of our service, following intelligently the several suffrages and Collects, perfectly conscious of their meaning as they were uttered, and yet we might not have made one single prayer our own. Looking over a prayer is not the same as offering it.

Again, wishing for God's grace, or for any of those gifts which are the subjects of prayer, is not praying. Some of these we cannot but wish for, if we are paying attention while they are mentioned. And yet we do very often think and speak about them without praying for them.

A very simple case will shew how far these fall short of prayer.

Suppose then a child who has made his father angry by some offence, and who shortly after, while the sense of his father's displeasure and the fear of punishment are strong within him, wants some indulgence, and yet dares not ask for it. That child will feel, as keenly as if he were under no restraint, perhaps even more keenly, how much advantage or pleasure that indulgence would bring him. He will desire it eagerly, perhaps more eagerly than if there were no obstacle to its enjoyment. And yet perhaps he will say that he cannot ask for it. There are two difficulties; first the difficulty of facing his father, and then that of asking the favour and risking refusal or even reproof.

And so it is with the rebellious sons of our heavenly Father. They often long for the blessings which He has to bestow, and yet cannot bring themselves to seek Him out and ask for them. How many a man is weary of the burden of some besetting sin, and has ceased to feel any pleasure in the indulgence of it, who yet continues to practise it, because he cannot (or thinks he cannot) come in lowly self-abasement to the Throne of Grace, and cast his burden there.

Praying, then, implies seeking the presence of God. This is the first essential requisite. It is not my purpose now to point out how to do this, lest you should confuse the thing itself with any one of the various ways by which men have pursued it. But in this by some means or other you must succeed if you would pray. You must realize the presence of Him to whom you pray. You must speak as to a living being whose eye is upon you and who reads your heart.

But again: in prayer it is also necessary that you should distinctly ask of God whatever you want. You must not merely give some vent to your feelings, but must pour them out in address to Him. Yours must be the language not of passionate excitement spoken into the air, but of childlike reverence and earnest supplication. You must not shrink from telling Him your wants, your desires, your difficulties, your dangers, as you would tell them if with your bodily eye you could see Him as a parent. You must not draw back just when you have reached the presence-chamber, but you must go on and state your case. And then you will have prayed.

II. Secondly, let us ask, Why is it necessary to pray?

It is necessary in order that our souls may be kept alive. Prayer is the breath of the soul's life. Without it, our souls must be either dead or in a death-like trance. Acts of prayer are to the soul what the inhaling of fresh air is to the body. Of what avail is that fresh air to a corpse which cannot drink it in? And of what use is the constant presence of the Holy Spirit of God, if our souls cannot receive Him? We cannot tell of course how long a cessation from acts of prayer will kill the soul. God only knows. But it is dangerous to trifle in a matter of life and death; and this is a matter of life and death. Every moment that the dying man omits to breathe, it becomes the more likely that he will never breathe again. And every day which you let pass without a prayer makes it the more likely that you are losing the power to pray.

This, however, is not the only use of prayer. It is necessary not only for its effect upon ourselves, but also (I say it reverently) for its effect upon God. It is His appointed ordinance by which we are to expect to gain from Him whatever gifts we need. He has promised to answer it—not always in the way we expect, but in His own way, in the way which He knows to be "most expedient for us."

I do not pretend to explain why He, who knows our necessities before we ask, should have desired us "by prayer and supplication" to make our requests known unto Him. It is enough for us to know that He has attached to the promise that He will supply our wants this condition, that we ask for what we want. Prayer is necessary, if for no other reason, because He has enjoined it.

But you may say, Prayer is necessary, no doubt, to those who seek for spiritual blessings; but what has it to do with our obtaining those things which are requisite and necessary for the body? The sun rises on the evil and on the good; rain is sent on the just and on the unjust. We do not find that those who pray most instantly are most free from worldly troubles, and losses, and sorrows. It is true, God does not pledge Himself to let all things happen as they might choose. But He does promise to make "all things work together" for their good.

G

Whilst he who gains the good things of this
life without asking for them, or enjoys them
without thanking the Giver, will surely be a
loser by them at last; the man of prayer, on the
other hand, is taught of God to take them, if
they are vouchsafed to him, as the gifts of God
to be used for Him, and to be patient without
them if they are held back, in confidence that it
was not good for him to have them. He therefore has, in fact, the most who can feel that what
he has is sent in answer to his prayers. He and
he alone has *enough*.

Still, under the Christian dispensation, prayers
for spiritual blessings should predominate. And
here, too, we may be disappointed of the particular grace or blessing which we sought. It
may please God to subject us to more severe
temptation than we expected, or to hold back
from us that comfort of the soul for which we
longed. Yet His answer to our prayers is certain, as certain as it is that He will not give us
that for which we do not ask.

III. And now, my brethren, let me put to
you the third question. What hinders us from
praying? Let each be very honest with himself
in answering this question: it is a very mo-

mentous one. I can only suggest a few general heads under which our principal hindrances may in the main be reckoned. You can appropriate, each to himself, those which you know to belong to you. May God help you to be resolute in ascertaining the truth, and in acting upon it when you are clear what your case is!

1. The first hindrance that suggests itself is, that *we do not feel the need of prayer.* We are very well satisfied with things as they are; or, if we are dissatisfied, it does not occur to us that we should refer to God to improve them. The world and the things of the world occupy the whole of our minds and hearts, and we have no wish to think about those things which we know only by faith.

This temptation besets persons of all ages in various forms. To you, my brethren, it occurs probably in the form of an eager thirst for pleasures and amusements, and a capacity for enjoying them to the uttermost, which have deserted older people, and which they are often surprised to observe in you. Each day brings its tasks, irksome perhaps and distasteful, which you perform it may be conscientiously, it may be with as little trouble as you can or dare apply to them. Each day brings also its excitement and its pleasures, to which you turn with all the eagerness of youth, and which you enjoy with a never-failing appetite. That appetite is sustained by your intervals of work, to which you have no choice but to attend. Otherwise it would soon flag. But so long as you are school-boys it will not flag, and perhaps you feel even now that it makes too heavy demands upon you.

You know that its demands are too heavy, if they prevent you from ever thinking of your parents, or, we will say, writing home to them as often as they wish you to do so. And, believe me, its demands are too heavy also, if they keep your thoughts back from your heavenly Father, if they stand in the way of those continuous messages which you ought to be sending up to heaven.

Now what is more common among school-boys than this sort of thing? And yet, if I mistake not, there are times when each of you bethinks himself that all this is not quite right. Even in our early years the feeling will sometimes rise within us, at times of distress or disappointment, if not even in the very moment of success, that we were destined for something better and nobler than the mere business and amusements of this

world. At such moments you do feel the want
of some communion with the world unseen.
Never let them pass without a prayer.

2. Another very common hindrance to prayer
is that growing *sensation of independence* which is
so natural to those who are approaching manhood. You feel, as you grow older, that you
need not rely on others so much as you used to
do, that you are becoming more and more com-
petent to think for yourselves and to act for
yourselves. And this feeling, let me warn you,
natural and proper as it is to a certain extent, is
one which, from the opinions and sentiments
which are prevalent in our day, is only too
likely to become a dangerous snare to you. Indeed, there must at all times be a danger of self-
reliance which is in one sense a virtue becoming
a sin, by our mistaking our right to look upon
ourselves as independent of man's control for
a right to be independent of God. And I will
venture to say that if any of you have thus early
in your life made this mistake, you have had
opportunities of discovering that it is a mistake.
You have found that they who cannot bring
themselves to acknowledge their dependence
upon God soon lose their boasted independence,

soon find themselves the slaves of a harder master, the slaves of lust or vanity.

3. Another hindrance to prayer is *the presence of sin* permitted and encouraged in the heart. Nothing crushes the rising wish to feel after God and take shelter under His protection so soon or so fatally as any indulged habit of wilful sin. And on this subject I will speak plainly. There is no hope whatever of your learning to pray, unless you can make up your mind to cast out this inmate of your heart, whatever it be. It is painful to think how many deceive themselves by outward attention to the duties of religion, by observing forms of prayer, perhaps even by approaching the Lord's table from time to time, who yet allow some sinful feeling to reign within them, or some sinful habit to exercise a deadly influence over them, and who therefore know nothing of real communion between their souls and God.

Have I now said something which has touched the conscience of any one here present? Does this reveal to you the secret why you cannot pray? Oh! be sure of this. If you are the servant of sin in any form, nay more, if you incline unto wickedness with your heart, the Lord will not hear you. You may be uneasy, you may be miserable about yourself, you may cry out for fear; but your first prayer must be that God would give you grace to turn away from sin, or you will be unable to pray at all.

I had intended to say much more, to point out the difficulties which beset us, not only in our first attempts, but when we have fairly entered upon the task of learning to pray, and even when we have made some progress[a]. But time forbids me to do more than refer you to the "Directions concerning Infirmities," and the "Prayer against Failings," which have been left for the use of public school-boys by a great and holy public school-man, one who was brought up, as you are, in the habit of daily public prayer, and who doubtless knew by experience the same temptations to weariness or neglect with which (may I not venture to say so?) you are all familiar. You will find them at the end of that Manual of Prayers[b] which is daily, let me hope, in the hands of every one of you.

I had intended also to speak of another and a more cheering subject, the encouragements to

[a] See the following Sermon.
[b] Bishop Ken's Winchester Manual.

prayer. But it was better not to risk, by attempting too much, the danger of uttering mere generalities upon a subject upon which we are all only too ready to shrink from examining ourselves closely.

4. In conclusion, let me name one more hindrance to prayer, which is in fact the necessary consequence of those already specified, and the mention of which brings us back to the text from which we started. I mean *false notions of what God is*, and *of the light in which He regards us.* Learn, my dear brethren, not to think of Him as of an angry Lord, of whom you are afraid and from whom you turn in terror. Fear Him as you fear your earthly father, not with such fear as will drive you away from Him, but with that loving reverence which becomes a right-minded son, who, while he loves his father's presence, feels himself to be under some restraint there, and learns to like that feeling.

Here then we find the answer which our Lord gave to that disciple who besought Him, saying, "Lord, teach us to pray;" and which He will give to those of you who apply to Him with the same request. He will bid you to be bold in claiming the privilege of sons conferred upon you at your baptism. He will say, "When ye pray, say, Our *Father.*" "If ye" men "being evil know how to give good gifts unto your children, how much more shall your heavenly Father give the Holy Spirit *to them that ask Him?*"

May He teach you all to recognise and value your adoption. May He help you to cast out whatever makes you forget or doubt it. May He teach you your need of His continual help. May He shew you clearly how false is that spirit of so-called manliness which would despise His love. May He purge your hearts from all those evil influences which would turn you from Him, and scatter from before your eyes those black mists which conceal His loveliness. May He— as I know He will, if you will seek Him—encourage you to come boldly to the throne of His grace, seeking mercy and grace in every time of need.

SERMON VIII.

Impediments to Prayer.

[Twenty-fifth Sunday after Trinity.   Nov. 17, 1861.]

"LORD, TEACH US TO PRAY."—*St. Luke* xi. 1.

YOU may remember that, the last time I preached
to you, I made some remarks upon the nature
and necessity of prayer, and upon the reasons
why some men never pray at all.   I pointed out
to you that prayer must not be confused with the
mere cherishing of religious sentiments, or with
the wish to obtain the blessings of which we
stand in need.   These are necessary indeed, as
introductory to prayer; but they are only introductory.   And they may be found and may
exist for a long time in a heart which is a
stranger to the spirit of prayer.   Praying in-
volves, I told you, these two things—seeking
out the presence of the living God, and, when
we have presented ourselves before Him, pour-
ing out our supplication at His throne.   And I
shewed you, by the familiar example of a child

who has offended his father, that this is not
a mere fine-drawn distinction, but a very important difference.

We then considered the necessity of prayer;
first, because of its effect upon our own souls,
to whose life it is as essential as breathing is to
that of the body; and secondly, because of its
effect upon Him who has commanded us to pray,
and who has assured us that He is moved by the
prayers of the very humblest of us.

And then we glanced at some of the barriers
which keep men back from prayer—the engross-
ing attractions of the world, the desire to feel
ourselves independent, the deadening influence
of sinful habits, the forgetfulness of that relation
in which we stand to the heavenly Father who
has adopted us.

Let us now pursue the subject further. There
are, I told you, other impediments to prayer,
which make themselves felt not so much at first
as after we have made some progress in praying.
Let me to-day point out some of these, for which
you must be prepared.

I. Foremost among those hindrances of which
we are now to speak, I would place *the influence
of habits unfriendly to devotion.* I do not mean

such habits as are positively and unquestionably
sinful; of such we have already spoken. I am
now supposing the case of persons who have advanced far enough towards God to have given up
all wilful indulgence in sin. And I say that
even such persons will feel at times that many
things not wrong in themselves are doing their
souls an injury, are dragging them down to earth
when they attempt to soar to the throne of God's
grace. Indeed, it is scarcely possible to be honest
in self-examination without discovering that we
have allowed ourselves to be bound down by some
one or other of these fetters; the grasp of which,
unless we resist in time, will tighten gradually
but fatally.

It has been said too truly, "Perimus licitis[a]."
We are ruined by things perfectly allowable in
themselves.

Hence the necessity of self-control and even
self-denial, lest even the very best of the employments of this world, its noblest anxieties,
its purest pleasures, become a snare to us. Nothing
will do instead of constant self-control and frequent self-denial to save us from this danger.

[a] See Sir Matthew Hale's scheme for a diary, in Bishop
Burnet's Lives, p. 23, Bishop Jebb's edition.

No general rules can be laid down. At least, when they are trusted implicitly, they are more likely to mislead than to guide aright. What does harm to one person may be harmless and even beneficial to another. But every man who has begun to seek acquaintance with God is, and must be, subject to this temptation in some form or other. Whatever rules of conduct you adopt, whatever line of life you follow, however free you may be from the vices of the world or of the flesh, yet you will be thus tempted. Let the ground be ever so good and ever so well cultivated, when the good seed begins to grow up the thorns will grow as well, and it is their nature to grow faster than the good plant, and, unless they are kept down by constant attention, to choke it before it brings forth fruit.

I spoke in my last sermon of the danger of trying to be independent of any master; the danger of which I am now speaking is rather that of trying to serve two masters. We may be earnest in wishing to keep up our acquaintance with God, and yet not have learned the necessity of keeping under the lower parts of our nature and bringing them into subjection. To you, then, who desire and strive to pray, I say,

Do not forget to "watch unto prayer." Be on your guard against every employment or amusement which you find by experience to render you disinclined to prayer. I do not say give up such employments or amusements altogether; perhaps you cannot do so, or, if you can, ought not to do so; and if you did, something else would take their place. But "use this world as not abusing it," nor forgetful that the fashion of it passeth away. Use it; do not let it use you. Make it your servant; do not be enslaved to it. Keep it in its proper place, and then you will learn that it may be made not a hindrance but a help to devotion. It will furnish you with subjects for prayer, and with inducements to prayer.

> "The trivial round, the common task,
>   Would furnish all we ought to ask;
>   *Room to deny ourselves; a road*
>   *To bring us, daily, nearer God* [b]."

I will not now dwell on any particular ways in which this danger is likely to beset us. But, as my desire is to make you feel the reality of it, I cannot pass on without just pointing out one or two to shew what I mean, and to suggest others.

[b] Christian Year—Morning.

Fasting and almsgiving have been called the wings of prayer. Now the reverse of these may as applicably be compared to dead weights preventing our souls from mounting up to high communion with God. The habit of always indulging our bodily appetites,—not to excess, (that of course we all know is of itself sinful,) but as far as we have opportunity within the bounds of temperance,—this, little as we may be disposed to allow it, has a deadening effect upon our souls. Again, the habit of always spending upon ourselves whatever money may be at our disposal,— not of taking for our own purposes what does not honestly belong to us (that of course is in itself a sin), but of invariably gratifying self with what is fairly our own, and never considering the wants of others,—this, too, will inevitably make it hard to pray.

It is true that God who gave us food and wealth meant that we should enjoy them, and sees us enjoy them without grudging us such pleasure. But He meant that we should learn in them the lesson of self-control; and, if we fail to learn it, they will most certainly tend to separate us from Him.

The same may be said of all worldly business,

and, especially to boys, of pleasures and amusements. I will specify one—the habit, common
and becoming every year more common, of reading amusing and exciting books. There are probably some amongst you who know what it is to
be so engrossed in a story as to be unable to con-
centrate their thoughts on prayer; who have
allowed their minds to dwell on it up to the
chapel door, and then have found that it forced
itself upon them within the chapel. And has
such an occupation as novel-reading never eaten
out the life of your private prayers, or even induced you to omit them altogether?

II. But, to pass on to a second difficulty, this
hovering about the border-land between right
and wrong is not the worst, no, not with the
very holiest of us. All, without exception, pass
the border sometimes. I do not now allude to
wilful and deliberate falling away from God,—
that does not fall within my present subject,—
but to what are called sins of infirmity. Those
who are really earnest are liable to frequent, aye
and often very grievous *lapses into sin.* And
every such fall makes it very hard to keep up
our habits of prayer.

And, oh! with what malice does the tempter

suggest to us, at such times, that it is useless for us to pray, for "God heareth not sinners;" that it is useless to seek Him, for our sin is a proof that He will not be found of us. Do we not all know what this feeling is? Have we not sometimes yielded to it?

There may be among my hearers some who feel a strong desire to make acquaintance with God, but who seem to themselves to be excluded from His favour by the weakness or the wickedness of which they know themselves to be guilty, and which, whenever they try to pray, the enemy of their souls brings vividly before them in all its grossness. Now I would not say one word to make any one careless about relapsing into sin. Sin is always dangerous, but, thank God, the Gospel assures us that it is not without a remedy. "If we confess our sins, He is faithful and just to forgive us our sins, and to cleanse us from all unrighteousness." For "if any man sin, we have an Advocate with the Father, Jesus Christ the righteous; and He is the propitiation for our sins." Persevere in prayer, in spite of sin and failure, and that Advocate will raise His voice in your behalf. Your weakness will not turn His face away, but will make Him all the more tender in His care

for you, even as a shepherd despises not the lambs
of his flock, but carries them in his arms.

Do you believe this? This is that true faith
in Jesus Christ our Saviour of which we read so
much in the New Testament. Perhaps you find
it hard, after you have fallen into any sin, to
come before God's throne armed with this faith,
and to pray in the words which that same Jesus
has taught you, "Forgive us our trespasses."
Consider, then, whether the obstacle be not mere
pride, a haughty feeling of annoyance to find that
all your boasted intentions of keeping yourself
clear from sin are worth so little, and that, if
you come to God, you must come humbly and
without any pretensions of your own to plead;
you must be prepared over and over again to
acknowledge yourself sinning and God forgiving,
yourself provoking and God forbearing, yourself
encompassed with infirmities and your High-
Priest touched with the feeling of those infirmities and interceding to set you free.

III. A third difficulty arises from *coldness of
heart*, the want of any feeling of love to God, or
perhaps of desire for the blessings which He has
to give. No man while he remains in this world
will be altogether free from this. It will beset

the most advanced saint now and then; and the young Christian must of course expect to feel it very often. We may kneel down to pray, and find that prayer for this time seems impossible; that we cannot bring ourselves to be earnest about it; that all is vain and unreal. It may even be the case, my brethren, that this sort of thing is not occasional merely, but constant with us; that all our prayers are forced, and will not flow naturally; that we soon grow weary, soon exhaust ourselves.

Be it so. This only proves our need of prayer. We must not be impatient. We must go on stedfastly removing all obstacles of which we are conscious, exercising ourselves in prayer, and, above all, praying for the spirit of prayer. Prayer is itself the cure of this evil. And though that cure will not be perfectly wrought so long as we remain encompassed with the weakness of the flesh, yet those who follow the Apostle's advice to " continue instant in prayer," to " pray always," to " pray without ceasing," will feel the genial rays of the Sun of Righteousness kindling the flame of love in their hearts, and making them " fervent in spirit."

IV. On this subject, however, we must not

dwell. There is one more difficulty, which no
doubt all of us have felt, and on which I am
anxious to say a few plain words: I mean *the
difficulty of controlling our thoughts.*

Need I say that the influence of this should be
especially guarded against in this place, where
united services are so frequent, and where the .
worshippers are so young? Is there one amongst
you who ever tried to give his earnest attention
to a whole service in chapel, who has not la-
mented, when it was over, the little power he
seemed to have of keeping his thoughts from
wandering?

Now, of course it would be very easy to reply
that this fact proves such constant services
to be ill adapted for you. But does it prove
this? Judge for yourselves. Do you find it
easier to keep your thoughts fixed upon the
service when you are at church elsewhere, when
perhaps you are joining in public worship only
on one day in the week? Could any one of you
say that the evil, whatever may be its strength
within him, is stronger here than in other places?
I doubt it. And with all my heart I urge you
never to cast the blame on others or on the system of the place, but to take whatever blame you

ought to take to yourselves. There is however, I believe, a fear of your blaming yourselves too much. "God does not require of us what we cannot do. There cannot be anything in these distractions to cut us off from His grace, unless they are wilfully encouraged and allowed. It is required of us that we should enter on every act of devotion with the intention of applying the mind to it seriously, and should not wilfully and knowingly depart from that intention°." And to those who thus purpose and thus strive God will not count it sin if they fail of absolute perfection, but will send His Holy Spirit to strengthen them. But be careful. You must be sincere : you must do your best. Then, and then only, you may expect His assistance. And I know no other cure.

But I do believe that much good may result from constant attendance on the services of our Church, which are so well arranged for catching the attention at intervals, if it has flagged, and for carrying us on from one occupation to another, from confession to praise, from praise to hearing the Word of God, and so on, without allowing any part of the service to be long and wearisome.

° Rev. Charles Marriott, Hints on Private Devotion, p. 94.

And therefore I recognise the wisdom of those who made the daily service part of our system of education here. They were not so simple as to suppose that you would be able always to keep your thoughts fixed upon the service, any more than a mother, when she first takes her child to church, expects that he will be able to understand and join in all that he sees and hears. But they did hope, and we do hope, and we do humbly pray, that by God's grace you would here train yourselves, or rather give yourselves up to God the Holy Spirit to be trained, in the habit of attention.

I do not say, Give yourselves up to us; for this is a matter in which we can give you no direct assistance. Indirectly we may help you, by the arrangements of our chapel and its services, by developing the spirit of our Church service and of our course of fasts and festivals, by checking such outward signs of carelessness as we have it in our power to restrain, and above all, by praying that God would take care of those His children who are here entrusted to us. But when we have given you the opportunity of learning to pray, it must rest with yourselves to use it or to neglect it.

Pray, then, with all your hearts, when we begin our service, that God would grant you "His Holy Spirit, that those things" "which we do at this present" may be so done as to please Him. Pray thus, but do not be content with praying. Strive also to keep yourselves mindful of His presence, and of the sacrifice which you have come to offer. For those who thus pray Christ Jesus will intercede. With those who thus strive the Holy Spirit will strive also. And though you may fall seven times a-day, yet He will raise you up and make your service acceptable.

The remarks which I will now bring to a close have been made under the impression that it would be a relief and an assistance to some of you to hear difficulties which you must have felt spoken of in plain terms, and without any attempt to make out that they are no difficulties at all. You are not mistaken in fearing them. Only remember that you are not the only persons who have been troubled by them; that they beset all the sons of God in turn; and that God, who allows them to stand in your way, has provided a remedy for them.

And so I invite you to approach to your Saviour frequently with the petition, "Lord, teach us to pray." And though He may try your patience by delay, yet He will answer you in time, as He answered that one of His disciples who addressed these words to Him. He will answer you by teaching you the relationship in which you stand to God. He will teach you when you pray to say, and to say with all your heart, " Our Father." He will encourage you to trust in Him, in spite of all your sinfulness and infirmity, because He knows them and feels a Father's sympathy with you in those difficulties which I have named, and in all others too.

For " like as a father pitieth his own children, even so is the Lord merciful unto them that fear Him. For He knoweth whereof we are made: He remembereth that we are but dust."

SERMON IX.

Holy Scripture a Rule for the Young.

[Fifth Sunday after Easter. May 25, 1862.]

" WHEREWITHAL SHALL A YOUNG MAN CLEANSE HIS
WAY: EVEN BY RULING HIMSELF AFTER THY WORD."
—*Psalm* cxix. 9.

IN this Psalm, which has just come round once
more in our monthly course, we find the Holy
Scriptures considered from almost every point of
view. The verse just read suggests them as
a guide and a safeguard against pollution for
those who are just entering upon life. And it
is my desire to say a few plain words on this
subject this morning.

If David esteemed the sacred writings to be
valuable for such a purpose, how much more
should we. For how small a portion of our
Bible was known to him. The Five Books of
Moses, and a few of the historical Books which
follow them, with the addition perhaps of the
Book of Job, constituted the whole of that "law"
or "word" of God to which he so constantly

refers. Yet they were sufficient to supply him with food for continual meditation, and to guide him infallibly upon the paths of holiness.

We who possess in addition that rich treasure which David himself has left us in his life and writings, who have before us the marvellous exhibition of God's omnipotence and of His forbearance which the later history of the Jews supplies and which the writings of the prophets so strikingly illustrate, we before whom the Gospel scheme has been unfolded, and to whom the words of our Lord and His Apostles are "as household words," are apt to set less store by the Holy Scriptures which are in our hands than David did by that small instalment of them to which he had access.

Yet we need instruction, we need guidance and reproof, and comfort and encouragement, as much as he did. The world has grown older and in some respects wiser, but certainly not so much wiser or so much better that the youth of our day can afford to dispense with the light which God offers them, or walk safely and uprightly with no other light than that of their own experience or their own wisdom. "Wherewithal shall a young man cleanse his way?"

There is only one true answer to the question now, as of old, "By ruling himself after" the Word of God.

Young men are not always disposed to *rule* themselves, or, as the Bible version has it, to "take heed" to their way at all. The one prominent circumstance, to their minds, about the time when they pass from boy to man, is the abrupt withdrawal of the restraints of boyhood. I say *abrupt;* because, however carefully and by whatever slow degrees we may remove those restraints one by one, yet there is a gulf which we cannot bridge over. There must be a day in your life (unless death prevent it) on which you will rise subject to the authority of others and lie down your own master. And when that sensation of freedom is first felt, how will you act? Are you prepared, are you preparing for the time when the voice of remonstrance or of warning, from parent or from tutor, must be silent, when you must act for yourself, and think for yourself? It is the business of this place to prepare you for this important crisis. Is that business being done? Are you becoming more and more manly, more fit to be a man?

To answer this question we must look again at

our text. "Wherewithal shall a young man cleanse his way? Even by ruling himself." Unless you are learning the lesson of self-control here, there is no solid reason for expecting that you will practise it hereafter. Circumstances are now more favourable for beginning to learn it than they will ever be again. Do not lose the opportunity.

But when you have determined not to yield the rein to passion or to impulse, you will not have done all. When you have decided on governing and restraining self, the further question must be asked, By what rule? And here, again, there is in the young a disposition to go astray. Fashion,—the general fashion of the day, or the particular fashion of some narrow circle,— public opinion, party spirit, all these and other rulers put their claims forward so loudly as not unfrequently to drown the "still small voice" of the rightful sovereign—conscience. It is not always an easy matter for young men, however well disposed, to yield themselves to this master. Let me then urge upon you the necessity of beginning at once to train it, and to subject yourself to it, and it to the law by which it is to govern—the law of God. And thus you may learn the secret of keeping clear from all pollution the way of your youth, even by learning to take heed to it according to the Word of God.

The train of thought which we have pursued thus far suggests one or two practical reflections which it is desirable to press upon you.

I. The first is *the importance of instruction in Holy Scripture.*

One very marked feature in the Church to which we belong is the care which she takes to make her members acquainted with the Word of God. You know how large a portion of our daily service (fully one half) consists of the simple words of Scripture. You know that those members of the Church who attend all her services regularly hear the whole Bible read through in the course of the year, with the exception of such portions as are not suited for public or cursory reading. And let me remark that this mere reading of God's Word in public without any comment or explanation ought to be regarded as a means of grace. It is too much the fashion to look upon sermons as the only public instruction of the Church. But our Church does not lay so much stress upon the words of her ministers as upon the words of God. The

Prayer-book provides lessons for every service, but orders a sermon for only one in the whole week. Mark that word *lessons*. Do not let the chapters which are read to you fall unheeded upon your ears because you know that you can read them in private if you like. God gives you the opportunity of hearing them, and expects you to learn something when you hear them. And depend upon it, he who listens in a teachable spirit will not grow tired of hearing the same words again and again, but will learn new lessons from them every time he hears them. There is a special blessing on that public reading, just as there is a special promise to public prayer.

The word "preach," as it is used in the New Testament, includes this public reading of the word just as much as the expositions or exhortations which the clergy found upon it. But then, in order that you may profit by this public reading of the Word, some previous instruction is necessary. Some passages of Scripture are "hard to be understood," and may be wrested to destruction. Hence the necessity of such teaching as that which you receive here every day. If that portion of our day's work were omitted we could not profess, as we do profess, to be training you in the principles of our scriptural Church. We do not, of course, suppose that we can explain to you all the difficulties of Holy Scripture : on some of them we should do wrong even to enter with persons of your early age. It would be impossible to make you understand exactly wherein the difficulty consists, and in many instances most undesirable to suggest to your minds subjects on which they are as yet not prepared to exercise themselves. Our object is to lay a good foundation for future study and for future edification; and that is an important part of education for all classes. Of course the method of instruction and the amount of instruction must differ with different circumstances. But low as well as high should be taught to love the Word of God, and to read it not carelessly or proudly, but humbly and with docility as the Word of God. And let me remind you of the appeal which is made to you to-day, to you who have such abundant opportunities of receiving this instruction, for help in extending it to the children of our neighbours who need our help, by the maintenance of their parochial school. But the care which, by God's blessing, will

suffice for them will not suffice for you. Well-
educated men ought to know more about their
Bible than the poor. I fear it frequently happens that they rest satisfied with an amount of
knowledge not greater, but far inferior. And
I want to warn you of the danger of resting
satisfied in future years with that acquaintance
with God's Word which you gain here, and of
failing to extend your reading or even to keep
it up. Such study of the Bible in our own and
the original languages ought not to be left to
the clergy. An eminent layman of our Church
wrote thus in the seventeenth century with re-
ference to the study of the Hebrew language:
"For my part, that reflect often on David's
generosity, who would not offer as a sacrifice
to the Lord his God that which cost him nothing, I esteem no labour lavished that illus-
trates or endears to me that divine book; my
addictedness to which I gratulate to myself, as
thinking it no treacherous sign, that God loves
a man, that He inclines his heart to love the
Scriptures, where the truths are so precious and
important that the purchase must at least de-
serve the price. And I confess myself to be
none of those lazy persons, that seem to expect

to obtain from God the knowledge of the won-
ders of His Book upon easy terms." These are
the words, not of a man of leisure, but of one
deeply engaged in philosophical and scientific
pursuits—of Robert Boyle[a].

The point on which I am insisting is this.
Those who have smaller opportunities of study
than you have may expect God's blessing upon
their reading as much as yourselves. He will
give them, as He will give you, sufficient light
to enable them to take heed to their paths, and
to keep them pure. But if you fail to use your
opportunities, if you omit the pains which, if
you loved His Word, you might take in the
study of that Word, what right will you have
to look for the help of His Holy Spirit to en-
lighten you?

II. I have dwelt so long upon this subject,
that I can only add a few words upon two others
equally important, and deserving of more ample
consideration. One is the necessity of not only
reading, but meditating on and applying to ourselves that Word of God which we read.

All that labour which it is possible to spend

[a] See a quotation from his Essay on the Scripture, in
Birch's Life, p. 101.

and desirable to spend in learning and throwing light upon the contents of Scripture will be lost, if we do not realize that the Book is addressed to us, that (strange as it may seem) those histories, those prophecies, those poems, those letters, which seem to be (and in fact are) connected with persons long since dead, and places far distant, and a state of society quite unlike our own, do yet, if we will let them, apply closely to us, and furnish every one of us with hints for his own guidance. That Book is "a great asylum open to all," open to all conditions and at all seasons. Whatever may be our diversities "of moral habit or natural disposition, of accidental state or artificial station, of advancement or default in holiness;" we shall find a provision for our wants and necessities in Holy Writ, if we sincerely and seriously enquire for it. "We, and such as we, are the very persons of whom Scripture speaks." It is marvellous that in a book of such a description, and such a compass, there should be such versatility; but there is. "The Word of God is quick," that is, full of life, "and powerful, and sharper than any two-edged sword, piercing even to the dividing asunder of soul and spirit, and of the joints

and marrow, and is a discerner of the thoughts
and intents of the heart." "Like the eye of
a portrait uniformly fixed upon us, turn where
we will," such is the piercing glance of the
Bible:—

> " Eye of God's word ! where'er we turn
>   Ever upon us ! thy keen gaze
> Can all the depths of sin discern,
>   Unravel every bosom's maze :
>
> Who that has felt thy glance of dread
>   Thrill through his heart's remotest cells,
> About his path, about his bed,
>   Can doubt what spirit in thee dwells ?
>
> ' What word is this ?   Whence know'st thou me ?'
>   All wondering cries the humbled heart,
> To hear thee that deep mystery,
>   The knowledge of itself, impart [b]."

And need I tell you that such use of God's
Word must be made upon our knees, must be accompanied by prayer? Indeed, whenever any
portion of the Bible is about to be read in public,
I would advise you to offer some short prayer

[b] Christian Year—St. Bartholomew's Day. Several expressions in the Sermon are borrowed from Miller's Bampton
Lectures; a passage in which appears to have suggested
these lines.

for grace to listen to and to profit by what is
read. But this enlightenment must be sought
also by private reading. I doubt not, God has
sometimes touched the conscience of every one
of you with some words of Scripture which you
have heard or read. Heeded or not, this voice
has spoken; for that is the way in which He
speaks to Christians. And here, where you are
in the habit of hearing and reading so much,
I may suggest to you that, when you are thus
impressed by any verse or chapter, impressed
perhaps without knowing why, you should at
night read over in private whatever has struck
you, and ask God to press the lesson home.
Such a practice would, I believe, do much to
strengthen you in the habit of listening for His
voice, and to bless for you the ministrations of
the Church.

III. In conclusion, I must say a few words
upon another subject. The Epistle for this day
has warned us of the fate of those who are only
hearers of the word and not doers. They deceive
themselves. The Word of God is indeed a glass
—a mirror in which each man may, as I have
said, discern his own features. But he who has
looked therein, and seen himself described there,

may go away and forget what manner of man he was. The engrafted word is able to save our souls, but only if it be engrafted and bring forth fruit in us. "Wherewithal shall a young man cleanse his way?" Not by reading the Word of God, not by making himself a familiar student or an able critic of it, but "by ruling himself after" it.

Take it as your guide; follow where you know that it would lead you. Be not deterred by fears of difficulty or of inconvenience, of persecution or of ridicule. Submit your judgment to it; believe what you know it tells you to believe; do what you know it bids you do; abstain from what you know it teaches you to hate.

During the next few years, my brethren, you will form your habits—habits which in all probability will rule you to the end of life. Form them according to this rule. Study it; meditate upon it; love it; obey it. You will find most assuredly, if you do so, that it will remove difficulties, save you from dangers, shield you from pollutions.

And as you advance in years, and reach that period of life when pleasure ceases to attract,

and worldliness begins to make its attacks upon
your allegiance, you will be rewarded by the
ability to repel this new foe, as you had kept off
before it the pollutions of youth. That same
Word which had kept clean your way in earlier
years will make you independent of what is
called success in life, that success which you all
anticipate, but which comparatively few of you
will gain. It will cause you more delight than
" all manner of riches." The law of God's
mouth will be "dearer unto you than thousands
of gold and silver."

SERMON X.

Church Principles.

[Whitsunday. June 8, 1862.]

" THERE IS ONE BODY, AND ONE SPIRIT, EVEN AS YE ARE
CALLED IN ONE HOPE OF YOUR CALLING ; ONE LORD,
ONE FAITH, ONE BAPTISM, ONE GOD AND FATHER OF
ALL, WHO IS ABOVE ALL, AND THROUGH ALL, AND IN
YOU ALL. BUT UNTO EVERY ONE OF US IS GIVEN
GRACE ACCORDING TO THE MEASURE OF THE GIFT OF
CHRIST."—*Ephesians* iv. 4—7.

THIS day is the birthday of the Christian
Church. During the forty days which elapsed
between Easter and the Ascension our Lord had
instructed His Apostles in the things pertaining
to that Church, or kingdom, as St. Luke tells
us[a]. And then having organized the body, He
left them to ascend to His Father's throne, and
to procure for it the breath of life, the most
Holy Spirit.

Ten days afterwards, God breathed into that

[a] Acts i. 3.

"one body" the "one Spirit;" and its never-
ending life began. I say *never-ending*, for though
particular members, when they have been proved
quite corrupt, may be severed from it, and may
lose the life which was transmitted to them
through it from the head, yet the body itself
lives on, uninjured and unmutilated by these
apparent losses ; nay, rather, increasing in beauty
and in stateliness as years go by, gaining both
by the addition of new members and the growing gracefulness of those already incorporated in
it, advancing steadily towards that state of glorious perfection in which it shall hereafter be presented by Christ its head to the Father, "not
having spot or wrinkle, or any such thing."

It is true that we do not see all this process
going on. So far as man can see and judge,
the history of the Church, like all other histories,
is a record in which sin and failure occupy
a prominent place. One cannot read it without
a feeling of shame that so much of unworthy
motive and pollution of this world should stand
unmistakeably printed even on its brightest pages,
and of amazement that its Head, after all that
He has done for it, can bear so patiently with
all its shortcomings. With regard especially to

that unity for which our Saviour prayed[b], and on which the Apostle dwells in the text with so much fervour, what can we say? We can but own that for centuries it has not been seen, and that, so far from its existence being a help to the world to believe that Christ was sent from God, the want of it is found to be the greatest obstacle to the propagation of the faith.

But though we do not *see* such unity as formerly gave to the words before us "a point and a reality which we know not," yet we *believe* in the unity of the Church. We "acknowledge one Catholic and Apostolic Church." Though, for our sin and faithlessness, the sight be hidden from our eyes; yet, as seen from the vantage-ground of God's throne on high, the body stands "fitly joined together and compacted by that which every joint supplieth," and is making increase daily.

How near or how distant its maturity may be, we know not. Nor can we tell how far the faithlessness or wilfulness of man, which has destroyed its outward unity, may also retard its growth. It is enough for us that its growth and perpetuity are absolutely promised; that

[b] John xvii. 20, 21.

"the gates of hell shall not prevail against" the
building which Christ has erected on the rock
which He has chosen; that that body, to which
He as the head imparts a share of His own life,
shall never see corruption or decay.

Out of this subject there arise many hard and
many painful questions, on which this is not the
place to enter. Yet the subject ought not therefore to be suppressed. We cannot conceal from
you the fact that Christians are divided. And
amid the strife of rival Churches and sects which
have boldly separated themselves from those
Churches, it would be wrong not to teach you
that there is still such a thing as Church unity.
Who are included in it, we cannot absolutely
decide. This is matter of faith, not of sight.
But we are bound to bring you up in the belief
that you share in it; and, thank God, there can
be no reasonable doubt of that. It is no concern of ours to judge other bodies of Christians:
God gives us light enough to judge ourselves,
but not light enough to judge others. And
when we profess to train you here on Church
principles, we mean not that we will teach you
to use hard words about other Churches and
their doctrines; but that we will try to promote

in you such habits, such convictions, and such
a tone of feeling as will, please God, enable you
all your life long to take comfort in applying to
our own branch of the Church that statement
of Christian truth which St. Paul here makes to
the Ephesians, and to endeavour to maintain
this "unity of the Spirit in the bond of peace."

For us, then, "there is one body, and one
Spirit, even as we are called in one hope of our
calling; one Lord, one faith, one baptism, one
God and Father of all, who is above all, and
through all, and in *us* all." We are not to regard ourselves as isolated individuals, but as
members united in one body. The same Spirit
from on high is breathed into all our hearts;
the same hope of salvation is held up before
all our eyes; the same Lord died for all; the
same faith has been taught to all, and is professed
daily in the Creed; the same Sacrament of
Baptism has been administered to all, to make
us sharers in this unity; the same God has
adopted us all, to cry to Him as children, "Our
Father."

But if Christians are not united amongst themselves, why put this doctrine forward? If we
could see this unity, no doubt it would be a help

and a comfort to us. But as we cannot, it would be better to say as little as possible about it, and to dwell on other doctrines more profitable and more practical. Many persons say this, and many others probably think the same, though they do not speak out. Many would be content to go on all their lives professing in the Creed that they believe in " the Holy Catholic Church" and " the Communion of Saints," and never thinking what that profession means; looking upon their religion as a matter which rests entirely between themselves and God, altogether a private thing with which no other man has anything to do. And not only so, but they too frequently look with suspicion and dismay on all attempts to teach these forgotten doctrines, and proclaim in no doubtful words that to do so is inconsistent with a due acknowledgment of our Saviour's merits and the Holy Spirit's influence.

With regard to the latter subject—which belongs especially to this day—St. Paul, as it seems to me, supplies a sufficient answer to the objection in the text. After stating so fully wherein the unity of the Church consists, he goes on immediately to enforce the truth that that same gift whose presence is the life of the Church is also given to each separate member of the Church, to preserve his life and to enable him to discharge his office. He places these side by side. He looks upon them not as contradictory to one another, nor even as rival truths, but as two parts of one and the self-same truth. It cannot then be true that they who love to dwell on this view of the Church necessarily substitute their Church for their Saviour, and spend that care on maintaining their union with the Church which should have been spent on guarding the presence of the Holy Spirit in their hearts. Nay, rather, Church principles, *if fairly taught and kept in their proper place*, are the best safe-guard against error and delusion respecting this greatest and best of the gifts of our ascended Lord to men.

To train boys in these Church principles was, you know, the leading purpose for which this College was founded. And I pray God that this great object—whether it be popular or unpopular with men—may never be lost sight of here. I desire this because it seems to me that, if the writings of St. Paul are true, this is the secret of success in education for those who are disposed to measure their success as they believe that God will measure it hereafter. Let me, then, conclude my last sermon at St. Columba's with a few plain words explaining how this can be, why we desire that you should adopt not that standard of Church principles which happens to be current and popular in our day, but that which you find to be the standard of the Prayer-book; why you should form your opinion of what Church unity ought to be, not from that sad spectacle of division which we see around us, but from that very different sight which the early Christians presented to the heathen of their day, and of which we find a picture in the New Testament.

I. And first we teach you thus, because God has taught us thus. When the Word of God ceases to contain such passages as the chapter from which our text is taken, or the twelfth chapter of the First Epistle to the Corinthians, then it will be quite time enough to listen to those who would have us believe that in teaching Church principles we are neglecting Gospel principles. The Bible teaches both. We have then the warrant of God for teaching both. And let men say what they will, and argue as they please, they cannot prove those doctrines false or dangerous which God has made prominent in

His Word, and on which He inspired the Apostles to found their exhortations to the virtues of the Christian life. We teach Church principles because God has taught them, and we believe God to be wiser than those who are afraid of them. Nor could we expect His blessing upon our work, if we suppressed some portions of His revealed truth under the idle pretext of taking better care of the rest.

II. But it is not difficult to see further reasons why it is good to dwell upon them. Look back to the time when you first came here, when the sense of loneliness was the strongest feeling in your hearts, almost overpowering you with its bitterness? Do you now feel lonely here? Have you not learned to look upon yourselves as a part of the College? And has not that been some relief to you? I should be sorry to doubt it, however strong that natural feeling of relief may be of which you are conscious when the restraints of school are laid aside for a time. Is there one of you who could wish now never to have been at St. Columba's? I hope not. Does it not seem to you that you have gained something here, something of dignity, something which entitles you to the sympathy and affection, and even respect, of many persons who, but for this association, would care nothing for you? Have you never felt it add to your self-respect?

So it is, though in an infinitely higher sense, if we would believe it, with our Church communion. All Churchmen are members one of another; and we may claim this fellowship with the very greatest and holiest who live or have lived in the Church. And the Church has something else to give you, to which that feeble illustration which I have borrowed affords no parallel—a share in the presence of the Holy Spirit. He, great and holy as He is, cares for all, loves to dwell in all, even in the humblest of those who are members of the body of Christ. That membership which was conferred upon you at your Baptism is a "pledge to assure" you of this. It gives you a claim upon Him which He never fails to recognise. The promise that He will abide in you for ever is indeed not absolute, like the promise to the Church at large; it is conditional upon your using the gift He brings, and growing in holiness. But if it fail, the failure will be from no diminution of His love, no exhaustion of His grace.

Here is ample supply for that craving after sympathy which is natural to us all. Church privileges diligently used and improved will bring this home to us, as nothing else can. In the hour of solitude, or sorrow, or bereavement, aye, and even when we have fallen into sin, if we do but lift up our hearts to God, we may find comfort in those simple and familiar words, " I believe in the Holy Ghost, the holy Catholic Church, the communion of saints, the forgiveness of sins."

III. There is another purpose which Church principles serve, on which I must say a few words. They supply a wholesome check to that desire of advancement and distinction which is indeed natural to us, but which, if allowed to gain too much power over our hearts, becomes inevitably a sin and a snare. In the history of the world, who have done so much mischief as those who have laid themselves out for glory? in the history of the Church, who have wrought so much confusion as those who have allowed themselves to be overcome by a love of power or pre-eminence?

Natural and proper and valuable as the desire of advancement and of the good opinion of others

K

is to us all, yet it must not hold the first place.
It is natural and right that you should now
desire the distinction of School Prizes°. It will
be natural and right, and the duty of some of
you hereafter, to compete for College honours.
It will be natural and right, and the duty of
all of you to do your best, in whatever state of
life you may be placed; and one great motive
to doing our best is a desire of the approbation
of others. But once begin to pursue any of
these common objects of ambition (whether con-
sciously or unconsciously) for its own sake, once
make the attainment of them or of any one of
them your primary object in life, and besides
the necessary disappointment which will ensue,
disappointment if you fail, and perhaps still greater
disappointment if you succeed and prove how
little is the intrinsic value of that which cost
you so much,—besides this, you will have fallen
into idolatry; and the certain result will be
the common fate of all idolaters, degradation
both of intellect and heart.

May those who go forth from this place set
a nobler object before their eyes, and aim at

° Preached on the eve of the annual distribution of prizes
on St. Columba's Day.

a higher mark. The true dignity of man lies not in his own personal advancement, but in his union with Christ. Christ is the head; he is the member—it may be a very weak or lowly member, but he is set in the place for which he is best fitted, and has grace given to him, not to act as head but to do the duties of his station. Let duty then, the duty to which God calls us, and not glory, the glory which we ourselves should like, be our aim.

Then St. Columba's will have been successful,—and, O my dear boys, it rests with you to prove it,—not if we send out a great many eminent men, but if, as years go by, there be scattered here and there about the world a large and ever-increasing number of men who, wherever they may be,—in the Church, or in the College, or in the Courts, or in the barracks, or may be on the battle-field, in the crowded city or in the quiet and lonely country-place, in the familiar homes of our own land or far away across wide and distant seas,—are stimulated, by recollections of this quiet mountain-side, TO DO THEIR DUTY and TO GLORIFY THEIR GOD.

Theological and Devotional Works

JOHN HENRY AND JAMES PARKER,

OXFORD; AND 377, STRAND, LONDON.

New Books.

The Life of the Right Reverend Father in God, Thomas Wilson, D.D., Lord Bishop of Sodor and Man. Compiled, chiefly from Original Documents, by the Rev. JOHN KEBLE, M.A., Vicar of Hursley. In Two Parts, 8vo., 21s.

Sermons preached before the University of Oxford: Second Series, from M DCCC XLVII to M DCCC LXII. By SAMUEL, LORD BISHOP OF OXFORD, Lord High Almoner to the Queen; Chancellor of the Most Noble Order of the Garter. 8vo., *cloth*, 10s. 6d.

Sermons preached before the University of Oxford, and in Winchester Cathedral. By the late DAVID WILLIAMS, D.C.L., Warden of New College, Oxford, and Canon of Winchester; formerly Head Master of Winchester College. *With a Brief Memoir of the Author.* 8vo., *cloth*, 10s. 6d.

The Form of Sound Words : Helps towards holding it fast : Seven Sermons preached before the University of Oxford on some important points of Faith and Practice. By CHARLES A. HEURTLEY, D.D., Margaret Professor of Divinity, and Canon of Christ Church. 8vo., *cloth*, 7s. 6d.

An Exposition of the Lord's Prayer, Devotional, Doctrinal, and Practical; with Four Preliminary Dissertations, and an Appendix of Extracts from Writers on the Prayer for Daily Use. By the Rev. W. H. KARSLAKE, Fellow and sometime Tutor of Merton College, Oxford. 8vo., *cloth*, 7s. 6d.

The Ministration of the Spirit. Sermons preached on the Evening of each Wednesday and Friday during the Season of Lent, in the Church of St. Mary-the-Virgin, Oxford. By the LORD ARCHBISHOP OF YORK; Rev. PROF. MANSEL; Rev. DR. WORDSWORTH; Rev. T. L. CLAUGHTON, M.A.; Rev. Dr. STANLEY; Rev. T. T. CARTER, M.A.; the LORD BISHOP OF LONDON; Rev. J. R. WOODFORD, M.A.; Rev. DR. PUSEY; Rev. D. MOORE, M.A.; Rev. DR. MAGEE; Very Rev. DEAN ALFORD. 8vo., cloth, 7s. 6d.

963-(1)-25*   1

Commentaries, &c.

The Minor Prophets; with a Commentary Explanatory
and Practical, and Introductions to the Several Books. By the
Rev. E. B. PUSEY, D.D., Regius Professor of Hebrew, and Canon
of Christ Church. *4to., sewed, 5s.*

Part I. contains HOSEA—JOEL, INTRO- DUCTION.	Part III. AMOS vi. 6 to end—OBADIAH —JONAH—MICAH i. 12.
Part II. JOEL, INTRODUCTION—AMOS vi. 6.	Part IV. nearly ready.

*The Authenticity and Messianic Interpretation of the
Prophecies of Isaiah* vindicated in a Course of Sermons preached
before the University of Oxford, by the Rev. R. PAYNE SMITH,
M.A., Sub-Librarian of the Bodleian Library, and Select Preacher.
8vo., cloth, 10s. 6d.

A Plain Commentary on the Book of Psalms (Prayer-
book Version), chiefly grounded on the Fathers. For the use of
Families. 2 vols., *Fcap. 8vo., cloth,* 10s. 6d.

The Psalter and the Gospel. The Life, Sufferings, and
Triumph of our Blessed Lord, revealed in the Book of Psalms.
Fcap. 8vo., cloth, 2s.

A Plain Commentary on the Four Holy Gospels, intended
chiefly for Devotional Reading. 7 vols., *Fcap. 8vo., cloth,*
£1 8s. 6d.; *strongly bound,* £2 2s.

Short Notes on St. John's Gospel. Intended for the Use of
Teachers in Parish Schools, and other Readers of the English
Version. By HENRY DOWNING, M.A., Incumbent of St. Mary's,
Kingswinford. *Fcap. 8vo., cloth,* 2s. 6d.

Short Notes on the Acts of the Apostles. Intended for
the Use of Teachers in Parish Schools, and other Readers of the
English Version. By HENRY DOWNING, M.A., Incumbent of
St. Mary's, Kingswinford. *Fcap. 8vo., cloth,* 2s.

*A New Catena on St. Paul's Epistles to the Ephesians
and Philippians.* A Practical and Exegetical Commentary, in
which are exhibited the Results of the most learned Theological
Criticisms, from the Age of the Early Fathers down to the Present
Time. Edited by the late Rev. HENRY NEWLAND, M.A., Vicar
of St. Mary-Church, Devon, and Chaplain to the Bishop of Exeter.
8vo., cloth, 12s.

Commentaries of the Fathers, published in the Series of
the Library of the Fathers. *Vide page* 10 *of this Catalogue.*

Reflections in a Lent Reading of the Epistle to the Romans
By the late Rev. C. MARRIOTT. *Fcap. 8vo., cloth,* 3s.

2

PUBLISHED BY J. H. AND J. PARKER.

Ecclesiastical History, &c.

A History of the Church, from the Edict of Milan, A.D. 313, to the Council of Chalcedon, A.D. 451. By WILLIAM BRIGHT, M.A., Fellow of University College, Oxford; late Professor of Ecclesiastical History in the Scottish Church. *Post 8vo.*, 10s. 6d.

The Sufferings of the Clergy during the Great Rebellion. By the Rev. JOHN WALKER, M.A., sometime of Exeter College, Oxford, and Rector of St. Mary Major, Exeter. Epitomised by the Author of "The Annals of England." *Fcap. 8vo., cloth*, 5s.

The Ecclesiastical History of the First Three Centuries, from the Crucifixion of Jesus Christ to the year 313. By the late Rev. DR. BURTON. *Fourth Edition. 8vo., cloth*, 12s.

A History of the Church of England, to the Revolution of 1688. By the late Rev. J. B. S. CARWITHEN, B.D. A new Edition, edited by the Rev. W. R. BROWELL, M.A. 2 vols., *Fcap. 8vo., cloth*, 12s.

A Brief History of the Christian Church, from the First Century to the Reformation. By the Rev. J. S. BARTLETT. *Fcap. 8vo., cloth*, 2s. 6d.

St. Paul in Britain; or, The Origin of British as Opposed to Papal Christianity. By the Rev. R. W. MORGAN. *Crown 8vo., cloth*, 4s.

The Councils of the Church, from the Council of Jerusalem, A.D. 51, to the Council of Constantinople, A.D. 381; chiefly as to their Constitution, but also as to their Objects and History. By the Rev. E. B. PUSEY, D.D. *8vo., cloth*, 10s. 6d.

The Empire and the Church, from Constantine to Charlemagne. By Mrs. HAMILTON GRAY. *Crown 8vo., cloth*, 12s.

A History of the so-called Jansenist Church of Holland; with a Sketch of its Earlier Annals, and some Account of the Brothers of the Common Life. By the Rev. J. M. NEALE, M.A., Warden of Sackville College. *8vo., cloth*, 5s.

The Western World Revisited. By the Rev. HENRY CASWALL, M.A., Vicar of Figheldean, and one of the late Deputation to the United States. *Fcap. 8vo., cloth*, 3s.

Scotland and the Scottish Church. By the Rev. H. CASWALL, M.A., Vicar of Figheldean, Wilts.; Author of "America and the American Church," &c. *Fcap. 8vo., cloth*, 2s. 6d.

Biographies, &c.

A Few Notes from Past Life: 1818—1832. Edited, from Correspondence, by the Rev. FRANCIS TRENCH, M.A., Rector of Islip, Oxon. *Post 8vo., cloth gilt,* 7s. 6d.

Life of John Armstrong, D.D., late Lord Bishop of Gra-hamstown. By the Rev. T. T. CARTER, M.A., Rector of Clewer. With an Introduction by SAMUEL, LORD BISHOP OF OXFORD. *Third Edition. Fcap. 8vo., with Portrait, cloth,* 7s. 6d.

Memoir of Joshua Watson, Edited by EDWARD CHURTON, Archdeacon of Cleveland. *A new Edition, just ready.*

Footprints on the Sands of Time. BIOGRAPHIES FOR YOUNG PEOPLE. Dedicated to her Nephews and Nieces by L. E. B. *Fcap. 8vo., limp cloth,* 2s. 6d.

The Life and Contemporaneous Church History of Antonio de Dominis, Archbishop of Spalatro, which included the Kingdoms of Dalmatia and Croatia; afterwards Dean of Windsor, Master of the Savoy, and Rector of West Ilsley in the Church of England, in the reign of James I. By the late HENRY NEWLAND, D.D., Dean of Ferns. *8vo., cloth, lettered,* 7s.

The Prayer-book.

The Principles of Divine Service; or, An Inquiry concerning the True Manner of Understanding and Using the Order for Morning and Evening Prayer, and for the Administration of the Holy Communion in the English Church. By the Rev. PHILIP FREEMAN, M.A., Vicar of Thorverton, Prebendary of Exeter, and Examining Chaplain to the Lord Bishop of Exeter. 2 vols., *8vo., cloth,* 1l. 4s.

The concluding portion, on the Order for the Holy Communion, besides its proper subject, enters incidentally into most of the great religious questions of the day; as Atonement, Sacrifice, the Origin of the Sabbath-day, &c.

For those who have Vol. I. the price of Vol. II., with Introduction, will be 14s.; without the Introduction, 8s.

A History of the Book of Common Prayer, and other Authorized Books, from the Reformation; and an Attempt to ascertain how the Rubrics, Canons, and Customs of the Church have been understood and observed from the same time: with an Account of the State of Religion in England from 1640 to 1660. By the Rev. THOMAS LATHBURY, M.A. *Second Edition, with an Index. 8vo.,* 10s. 6d.

Articuli Ecclesiæ Anglicanæ; or, The Several Editions of the Articles of the Church of England, as agreed upon in Convocation, and set forth by Royal Authority, during the Reigns of King Edward VI. and Queen Elizabeth, arranged in one Comparative View. By WILLIAM HARRISON DAVEY, M.A., Vice-Principal of Cuddesdon Theological College, in the Diocese of Oxford. *8vo., cloth,* 2s. 6d.

Doctrinal Theology.

Inspiration and Interpretation. Seven Sermons preached before the University of Oxford; with an Introduction, being an answer to a Volume entitled "Essays and Reviews." By the Rev. JOHN W. BURGON, M.A., Fellow of Oriel College, and Select Preacher. *8vo., cloth,* 14s.

Discourses on Prophecy. In which are considered its Structure, Use, and Inspiration; being the substance of Twelve Sermons preached in the Chapel of Lincoln's Inn, by JOHN DA-VISON, B.D. *Sixth and Cheaper Edition. 8vo., cloth,* 9s.

Cur Deus Homo, or Why God was made Man; by ST. ANSELM, sometime Archbishop of Canterbury. Translated, with an Introduction containing some Account of the Author, and an Analysis of the Work, by A CLERGYMAN. *Second Edition. Fcap. 8vo.,* 2s. 6d.

The History of Popish Transubstantiation. By JOHN COSIN, D.D., Lord Bishop of Durham. A new Edition, revised, with the Authorities printed in full length. *Fcap. 8vo.,* 5s.

The Power of the Keys; or, Considerations on the Absolving Power of the Church, and upon some of the Privileges of the Christian Covenant. By the late Rev. DR. BURTON, Regius Professor of Divinity, and Canon of Christ Church, Oxford. *Second Edition. 8vo.,* 3s.

The Real Presence of the Body and Blood of our Lord Jesus Christ the Doctrine of the English Church; with a Vindication of the Reception by the Wicked, and of the Adoration of our Lord Jesus Christ. By E. B. PUSEY, D.D. *8vo., cloth,* 9s.

The Doctrine of the Real Presence, as set forth in the works of DIVINES and others in the English Church since the Reformation. *8vo., cloth,* 9s.

On Eucharistical Adoration. By the Rev. JOHN KEBLE, M.A., Vicar of Hursley. *Second Edition. 8vo.,* 3s. 6d.

Practical Theology.

Addresses to the Candidates for Ordination on the Questions in the Ordination Service. By SAMUEL, LORD BISHOP OF OXFORD, Chancellor of the Most Noble Order of the Garter, and Lord High Almoner to Her Majesty the Queen. *Fifth Thousand, Crown 8vo., price* 6s. *cloth.*

Parochial Work. By the Rev. E. MONRO, M.A., Incumbent of Harrow Weald, Middlesex. *Second Edition. 8vo., cloth,* 10s. 6d.

Letters from a Tutor to his Pupils. By the Rev. W. JONES, of Nayland. Edited by the Rev. EDWARD COLERIDGE, Under Master of Eton College, 18mo., *cloth,* 2s. 6d.

5

THEOLOGICAL AND DEVOTIONAL WORKS,

Devotional Works.

Ancient Collects and other Prayers, Selected for Devotional Use from various Rituals, with an Appendix on the Collects in the Prayer-book. By WILLIAM BRIGHT, M.A., Fellow of University College, Oxford, Author of "A History of the Church," &c. *Second Edition, enlarged. Fcap. 8vo., in red and black, on toned paper, price 5s.*

Daily Steps Towards Heaven. A small pocket volume containing a few PRACTICAL THOUGHTS on the GOSPEL HISTORY, with Texts for every Day in the Year, commencing with Advent. *Eleventh Edition. Bound in roan, 2s. 6d.*

An Edition in large type for the use of aged persons, square Crown 8vo., cloth, 5s.

Liturgia Domestica : Services for every Morning and Evening in the Week; for THE USE OF FAMILIES. *Third Edition, revised and enlarged. 18mo., 2s.*

Thoughts During Sickness. By the Author of "The Doctrine of the Cross," and "Devotions for the Sick Room." *Second Edition.* Price 2s. 6d.

The Pastor in his Closet; or, A Help to the Devotions of the Clergy. By JOHN ARMSTRONG, D.D., late Lord Bishop of Grahamstown. *Third Edition. Fcap. 8vo., cloth, 2s.*

Arden's Breviates from Holy Scripture. Arranged for use by the Bed of Sickness. By the Rev. G. ARDEN, M.A. *Second Edition. Fcap., cloth, 2s.*

The Cure of Souls. By the Rev. G. ARDEN, M.A., Rector of Winterborne-Came, and Author of "Breviates from Holy Scripture," &c. *Fcap., cloth, 2s. 6d.*

Lent Readings from the Fathers. Selected from "The Library of the Fathers." *Fcap. 8vo., cloth, 5s.*

Devotions for a Time of Retirement and Prayer for the Clergy. As used in the Diocese of Oxford. *Fcap. 8vo., 1s.*

The Threshold of the Sanctuary. A Devotional Manual for Candidates for Holy Orders. By the Rev. E. D. CREE, M.A. *16mo., limp cloth, 2s.*

Preces Privatæ in studiosorum gratiam collectæ et regia auctoritate approbatæ: anno MDLXVIII. *Londini* editæ: ad vetera exemplaria denno recognitæ. Ed. C. MARRIOTT. *16mo., cloth, 6s.*

6

Oxford Editions of Devotional Works.

IMITATION OF CHRIST.
FOUR BOOKS. By THOMAS À KEM-
PIS. A new Edition, revised, hand-
somely printed in fcap. 8vo., with
Vignettes and red borders. *Cloth, 5s.;*
antique calf, red edges, 10s. 6d.

LAUD'S DEVOTIONS.
THE PRIVATE DEVOTIONS of Dr.
WILLIAM LAUD, Archbishop of Canterbury, and Martyr. A new and revised Edition, with Translations to the
Latin Prayers, handsomely printed
with Vignettes and red lines. *Fcap.*
8vo., cl. antique, 5s.; bound, 10s. 6d.

WILSON'S SACRA PRIVATA.
THE PRIVATE MEDITATIONS,
DEVOTIONS, and PRAYERS of the
Right Rev. T. WILSON, D.D., Lord
Bishop of Sodor and Man. Now first
printed entire. From the Original
MSS. *Fcap. 8vo., antique cloth,* 4s.

ANDREWES' DEVOTIONS.
DEVOTIONS. By the Right Rev.
LAUNCELOT ANDREWES. Translated
from the Greek and Latin, and arranged anew. *Fcap. 8vo., antique*
cloth, 5s.; antique calf, red edges,
10s. 6d.

SPINCKES' DEVOTIONS.
TRUE CHURCH OF ENGLAND
MAN'S COMPANION IN THE
CLOSET; or, A complete Manual of
Private Devotions, collected from the
Writings of eminent Divines of the
Church of England. By NATHANIEL
SPINCKES. *Fcap. 8vo., floriated bor-*
ders, cloth antique, 4s.

TAYLOR'S HOLY LIVING.
THE RULE AND EXERCISES OF
HOLY LIVING. By BISHOP JE-
REMY TAYLOR. In which are described the means and instruments
of obtaining every virtue, and the remedies against every vice. *Antique*
cloth, 4s.

TAYLOR'S HOLY DYING.
THE RULE AND EXERCISES OF
HOLY DYING. By BISHOP JE-
REMY TAYLOR. In which are de-
scribed the means and instruments
of preparing ourselves and others re-
spectively for a blessed death, &c.
Antique cloth, 4s.

ANCIENT COLLECTS.
Lately published. Vide p. 6.

Church Poetry.

THE CHRISTIAN YEAR. Thoughts in Verse for the Sundays
and Holydays throughout the year.
Octavo Edition,—Large type, *cloth,* 10s. 6d.; *morocco, by Hayday,*
21s.; *antique calf,* 18s.
Foolscap Octavo Edition,—Cloth, 7s. 6d.; *morocco,* 10s. 6d.; *morocco*
by Hayday, 15s.; *antique calf,* 12s.
18mo. *Edition,—Cloth,* 6s.; *morocco,* 8s. 6d.
32mo. *Edition,—Cloth,* 3s. 6d.; *morocco, plain,* 5s.; *morocco, by*
Hayday, 7s.
Cheap Edition,—Cloth, 1s. 6d.; *bound,* 2s.
LYRA INNOCENTIUM. Thoughts in Verse for Christian Children.
Fcap. 8vo., cloth, 7s. 6d.; *morocco,* 10s. 6d. 32mo. *Edition,—Cloth,*
3s. 6d.; *morocco, plain,* 5s.; *morocco, by Hayday,* 7s.
Cheap Edition,—Cloth, 1s. 6d.; *bound,* 2s.
MORNING THOUGHTS. By a CLERGYMAN. Suggested by the
Second Lessons for the Daily Morning Service throughout the
Year. 2 vols. *Foolscap 8vo., cloth,* 5s. *each.*
THE CHILD'S CHRISTIAN YEAR. Hymns for every Sunday
and Holyday throughout the Year. *Cheap Edition,* 18mo., *cloth,* 1s.

7.

THEOLOGICAL AND DEVOTIONAL WORKS,

Church Poetry—continued.

FLORUM SACRA. By the Rev. G. HUNT SMYTTAN. *Second Edition.* 16mo., 1s.

THE CATHEDRAL. 32mo., with Engravings, 4s. 6d. *Fcap. 8vo., Eighth Edition*, 7s. 6d.

THOUGHTS IN PAST YEARS. *The Sixth Edition*, with several new Poems, 32mo., *cloth*, 4s. 6d.

THE BAPTISTERY; or, The Way of Eternal Life. 32mo., *cloth*, 3s. 6d.
The above Three Volumes uniform, neatly bound in morocco, 32mo., 18s.

THE CHRISTIAN SCHOLAR. *Foolscap 8vo.*, 10s. 6d. 32mo., *cloth*, 4s. 6d.

THE SEVEN DAYS; or, The Old and New Creation. *Fcap. 8vo., new Edition, cloth*, 7s. 6d.

CHRISTIAN BALLADS AND POEMS. By the Rev. A. C. COXE. 18mo. *A New Edition, with additions, just published,* price 3s.

DREAMLAND, and other Ballads, in a packet of 12 for One Shilling.

EPITAPHS FOR COUNTRY CHURCHYARDS. Collected and arranged by AUGUSTUS J. C. HARE. *Fcap. 8vo., cloth*, 2s. 6d.

HYMNS FROM THE GOSPEL OF THE DAY, for each Sunday and the Festivals of our Lord. By the Rev. J. E. BODE, M.A., Rector of Westwell, Oxon.; Author of Ballads from Herodotus, Bampton Lectures, &c. 18mo., 1s.

THE CLEVELAND PSALTER. The Book of Psalms in English Verse, and in Measures suited for Sacred Music. By E. CHURTON, M.A., Archdeacon of Cleveland. *Foolscap 8vo., cloth*, 7s. 6d.

PSALMODY FOR THE CHRISTIAN SEASONS, selected from the CLEVELAND PSALTER. 16mo., 1s.

ENGLISH HYMNAL. A Hymn-book for the Use of the Church of England. *Third Edition.* 18mo., *cloth*, 1s.

A COLLECTION OF ANTHEMS used in the Cathedral and Collegiate Churches of England and Wales. By W. MARSHALL, Mus. Doc. *A New Edition*, 12mo., *cloth*, with Appendix, 3s.

8

Catechetical Lessons.

Designed to aid the Clergy in Public Catechising. *Fcap. 8vo.*

I. THE APOSTLES' CREED. 6d.
II. THE LORD'S PRAYER. 6d.
III. THE TEN COMMANDMENTS. 6d.
IV. THE TWO SACRAMENTS. 6d.
V. THE PARABLES. Part I. 1s.
VI. THE PARABLES. Part II. 1s.
VII. THE THIRTY-NINE ARTICLES. 1s. 6d.

VIII. THE MORNING AND EVENING PRAYER, AND THE LITANY. 1s.
IX. THE MIRACLES OF OUR LORD. Part I. 1s.
X. THE MIRACLES OF OUR LORD. Part II. 1s.
XI. ON THE SAINTS' DAYS. 1s.

Now publishing, in Monthly Volumes, with a Frontispiece, price 1s.

A NEW SERIES OF

HISTORICAL TALES,

Illustrating Church History,

Adapted for General Reading, Parochial Libraries, &c.

England. Vol. I.

No. 1.—The Cave in the Hills; or, Cæcilius Viriäthus.
No. 14. — The Alleluia Battle; or, Pelagianism in Britain.
No. 5.—Wild Scenes amongst the Celts.
No. 7.—The Rivals : a Tale of the Anglo-Saxon Church.
No. 10.—The Black Danes.

England. Vol. II.

No. 21.—The Forsaken; or, The Times of St. Dunstan.
No. 18.—Aubrey De L'Orne; or, The Times of St. Anselm.
No. 16.—Alice of Fobbing; or, The Times of Jack Straw and Wat Tyler.
No. 24.—Walter the Armourer; or, The Interdict.
No. 27.—Agnes Martin; or, The Fall of Cardinal Wolsey.

America and our Colonies.

No. 3.—The Chief's Daughter; or, The Settlers in Virginia.
No. 8.—The Convert of Massachusetts.
No. 20.—Wolfingham; or, The Convict-Settler of Jervis Bay.
No. 25.—The Catechumens of the Coromandel Coast.
No. 28.—Rose and Minnie; or, The Loyalists : a Tale of Canada in 1837.

France and Spain.

No. 2.—The Exiles of the Cebenna; a Journal written during the Decian Persecution.
No. 22.—The Dove of Tabenna; and The Rescue.
No. 23.—Larache : a Tale of the Portuguese Church in the Sixteenth Century.
Two more Tales will shortly be issued to complete this volume.

Eastern and Northern Europe.

No. 11.—The Conversion of St. Vladimir; or, The Martyrs of Kief.
No. 17.—The Northern Light : a Tale of Iceland and Greenland.
No. 13.—The Cross in Sweden; or, The Days of King Ingi the Good.
No. 6.—The Lazar-House of Leros : a Tale of the Eastern Church.
No. 26.—The Daughters of Pola : a Tale of the Great Tenth Persecution.

Asia and Africa.

No. 19.—Lucia's Marriage; or, The Lions of Wady-Araba.
No. 9.—The Quay of the Dioscuri : a History of Nicene Times.
No. 4. The Lily of Tiflis : a Sketch from Georgian Church History.
No. 12.—The Sea-Tigers : a Tale of Mediæval Nestorianism.
No. 15.—The Bride of Ramcuttah : a Tale of the Jesuit Missions to the East.

9

𝔏𝔦𝔟𝔯𝔞𝔯𝔶 of t𝔥𝔢 𝔉𝔞t𝔥𝔢𝔯𝔰.

	Subscribers' Price. £ s. d.
S. AUGUSTINE'S Confessions. *Fourth Edition* -	0 7 0
—— Sermons on the New Test. 2 vols. - -	1 1 0
—— Homilies on the Psalms. 6 vols. - -	2 16 6
—— —— on the Gospel and First Epistle of S. John. 2 vols. - - - -	1 2 6
—— Practical Treatises - - - -	0 12 0
S. CHRYSOSTOM on S. Matthew. 3 vols. - -	1 7 0
—— Homilies on S. John. 2 vols. - -	0 18 6
—— —— on the Acts. 2 vols. - -	0 16 0
—— —— on S. Paul's Epistles. 7 vols. in 6	3 0 0
—— —— on the Statues - - -	0 9 0
S. CYRIL'S Lectures on the Creed. *3rd Ed.* - -	0 8 6
S. CYPRIAN'S Works. 2 vols. *3rd Edition* -	0 17 0
S. GREGORY THE GREAT on Book of Job. 4 vols.	2 2 0
S. EPHREM'S Rhythms on the Nativity, and on Faith,— (From the Syriac) - - - -	0 10 6
S. ATHANASIUS. Against the Arians. 2 vols. *2nd Ed.*	0 15 0
—— Historical Tracts - - -	0 8 0
—— The Festal Epistles - - - -	0 4 6
TERTULLIAN'S Treatises. *2nd Edition* - -	0 12 0
S. JUSTIN MARTYR. *Just published* - -	0 6 0
Or the complete set, 41 vols. - - -	18 0 0

ORIGINAL TEXTS.

	£ s. d.
S. AUGUSTINI Confessiones - - -	0 7 0
S. CHRYSOSTOMI in Epist. ad Corinth. I. - -	0 10 6
—— ad Corinthios II. - - -	0 8 0
—— ad Romanos - - - -	0 9 0
—— ad Galatas et Ephesios - - -	0 7 0
—— ad Philipp., Coloss., Thessal. - -	0 10 6
—— ad Tim., Tit., Philem. - - -	0 8 0
—— ad Hebræos et Indices - - -	0 12 0
THEODORETI ad Romanos, Corinth. et Galat. -	0 8 0

Library of Anglo-Catholic Theology.

	£	s.	d.
BP. *ANDREWES'* Sermons. 5 vols.	1	15	0
———— Pattern of Catechistical Doctrine, &c.	0	5	0
———— Tortura Torti	0	6	0
———— Responsio ad Apol. Card. Bellarmini	0	6	0
———— Preces Privatæ. Gr. et Lat.	0	5	0
———— Opuscula Posthuma	0	4	0
———— Minor Works and Indices	0	6	0
BP. *BEVERIDGE'S* English Works. 10 vols.	3	10	0
———— Codex Canonum. 2 vols.	0	14	0
ABP. *BRAMHALL'S* Works. 5 vols.	1	15	0
BP. *BULL'S* Harmony on Justification. 2 vols.	0	10	0
———— Works on the Trinity. 3 vols.	0	15	0
BP. *COSIN'S* Works. 5 vols.	1	10	0
CRAKANTHORP'S Def. Eccl. Anglicanæ	0	7	0
FRANK'S Sermons. 2 vols.	0	10	0
BP. *FORBES'* Considerationes Modestæ. 2 vols.	0	12	0
BP. *GUNNING* on the Paschal, or Lent Fast	0	6	0
HAMMOND'S Practical Catechism	0	5	0
———— Minor Theological Works	0	5	0
———— Sermons. 2 Parts	0	10	0
HICKES' Treatises on the Priesthood. 3 vols.	0	15	0
JOHN JOHNSON'S Unbloody Sacrifice. 2 vols.	0	10	0
———— English Canons. 2 vols.	0	12	0
ABP. *LAUD'S* Works. Complete. 7 vols.	3	3	0
L'ESTRANGE'S Alliance of Divine Offices	0	6	0
MARSHALL'S Penitential Discipline	0	4	0
BP. *NICHOLSON* on the Catechism	0	6	0
BP. *OVERALL'S* Convocation-Book. 8vo.	0	5	0
BP. *PEARSON'S* Vindiciæ Ignatianæ. 2 vols.	0	10	0
THORNDIKE'S Works. Complete. 6 vols.	2	10	0
BP. *WILSON'S* Works. Complete. With LIFE, by Rev. J. KEBLE. 7 vols. (8 Parts)	3	3	0

Sermons.

ARMSTRONG.—Parochial Sermons. By the late Lord Bishop of Grahamstown. *Second Edition. Fcap. 8vo., cloth,* 5s.

———————— Sermons on the Fasts and Festivals. *Second Edition. Fcap. 8vo., cloth,* 5s.

BARKER.—Plain Sermons preached in Parish Churches. By the Rev. THOMAS BARKER, M.A., of Queen's College, Oxford; late Tutor of Codrington College, Barbados. *Post 8vo., cloth,* 6s. 6d.

BEVERIDGE.—Sermons on the Ministry and Ordinances of the Church of England. By Bishop BEVERIDGE. 12mo., *cloth,* 3s.

BURBIDGE.—Leamington College Sermons.—School Life.—Sermons preached in the Chapel of Leamington College. By THOMAS BURBIDGE, LL.D., Master of the College. *Fcap. 8vo., cloth,* 5s.

BURROWS.—Parochial Sermons, by the Rev. HENRY W. BURROWS, B.D., Perpetual Curate of Christ Church, St. Pancras. *Fcap. 8vo., cloth,* 6s.

———————— Second Series. *Fcap. 8vo., cloth,* 5s.

CHRISTIAN SEASONS.—Short and Plain Sermons for every Sunday and Holyday throughout the Year. Edited by the late BISHOP OF GRAHAMSTOWN. 4 vols., *Fcap. 8vo., cloth,* 16s.

————————. A Second Series of Sermons for the Christian Seasons Uniform with the above. 4 vols., *Fcap. 8vo., cloth,* 16s.

By a Writer in the Tracts for the Christian Seasons.

ILLUSTRATIONS OF FAITH.—EIGHT PLAIN SERMONS, by a Writer in the "Tracts for the Christian Seasons:"—Abel; Enoch; Noah; Abraham; Isaac, Jacob, and Joseph; Moses; The Walls of Jericho; Conclusion. *Fcap. 8vo., cloth,* 2s. 6d.

Uniform, and by the same Author,

PLAIN SERMONS ON THE BOOK OF COMMON PRAYER. *Fcap. 8vo., cloth,* 5s.

HISTORICAL AND PRACTICAL SERMONS ON THE SUFFER-INGS AND RESURRECTION OF OUR LORD. 2 vols., *Fcap. 8vo., cloth,* 10s.

SERMONS ON NEW TESTAMENT CHARACTERS. *Fcap. 8vo.,* 4s.

FAMILY READING.—Ninety Short Sermons for Family Reading, following the Order of the Christian Seasons. 2 vols., *Fcap. 8vo.,* 8s.

FRASER.—Parish Sermons. Second Series. By WILLIAM FRASER, B.C.L., Vicar of Alton, Staffordshire, and Domestic Chaplain to the Earl of Shrewsbury and Talbot. *Fcap. 8vo., cloth, red edges,* 3s.

Sermons—continued.

FURSE.—Sermons preached for the most part in the Churches of St. Mary and St. Matthias, Richmond, Surrey. By CHARLES WELLINGTON FURSE, M.A., of Balliol College; Curate of Christ Church, St. Pancras; and formerly Lecturer of St. George's Chapel, Windsor. *Post 8vo., cloth,* 6s.

HARSTON.—Sermons by the Rev. E. HARSTON, Rector of Tamworth. *8vo., cloth,* 10s. 6d.

HEATHCOTE.—Seven Sermons preached on the Sundays in Lent, and Easter-day, 1862. By GILBERT VYVYAN HEATHCOTE, Literate Priest; Curate in sole charge of Rushall, Diocese of Salisbury. *Crown 8vo.,* 2s. 6d.

HEURTLEY.—The Union between Christ and His People. By the Rev. C. A. HEURTLEY, D.D., Canon of Christ Church. *Second Edition. 8vo., cloth,* 5s. 6d.

———— Justification : Eight Sermons at Bampton's Lecture, 1845. *Second Edition. 8vo., cloth,* 9s.

HUNTINGTON'S Sermons for the Holy Seasons of the Church, with others on various subjects. *8vo., cloth,* 6s.

———— Second Series, *8vo., cloth,* 6s.

HUNTLEY.—The Year of the Church. A Course of Sermons by the late Rev. RICHARD WEBSTER HUNTLEY, M.A., sometime Fellow of All Souls' College, Oxford, &c.; with a short Memoir by the Editor, the Rev. SIR G. PREVOST, Bart., M.A. *Fcap. 8vo., cloth lettered,* 7s. 6d.

HUSSEY.—Sermons, mostly Academical. With a Preface, containing a Refutation of a Theory founded upon the Syriac Fragments of the Epistles of St. Ignatius. By the late Rev. ROBERT HUSSEY, B.D. *8vo., cloth,* 10s. 6d.

LENTEN SERMONS AT OXFORD.—A Series of Sermons preached on the Evening of each *Wednesday* and *Friday* during the Season of Lent, 1857. *8vo., cloth,* 14s. Separately, 1s. each.

———— The Series for 1859. *Fcap. 8vo., cloth,* 5s.

LEEDS.—Sermons preached at the Consecration of St. Saviour's, Leeds. *8vo., cloth,* 7s. 6d.

MANT.—The Man of Sorrows. The Mental Sufferings of our Lord and Saviour Jesus Christ during His Passion; considered in Five Discourses. By the Ven. Archdeacon MANT. *12mo., cloth,* 2s. 6d.

MARRIOTT.—Sermons preached before the University of Oxford, and in other places. By the late Rev. C. MARRIOTT, Fellow of Oriel College, Oxford. *12mo., cloth,* 6s.

———— Volume the Second. *12mo., cloth,* 7s. 6d.

13

Sermons—continued.

MARRIOTT.—Lectures on the Epistle of St. Paul to the Romans. By the late Rev. C. MARRIOTT, B.D., Fellow of Oriel College, Oxford. Edited by his Brother, the Rev. JOHN MARRIOTT. 12mo., cloth, 6s.

MATURIN.—Six Lectures on the Events of Holy Week. By WILLIAM MATURIN, M.A., Perpetual Curate of Grangegorman, Dublin. Second Edition, Crown 8vo., limp cloth, 2s. 6d.

MEYRICK.—The Wisdom of Piety, and other Sermons, addressed chiefly to Undergraduates. By the Rev. F. MEYRICK, M.A., Her Majesty's Inspector of Schools; Fellow of Trinity College; late Select Preacher before the University of Oxford; and Her Majesty's Preacher at Whitehall. Crown 8vo., 4s.

MOBERLY. — Sermons on the Beatitudes, with others mostly preached before the University of Oxford; to which is added a Preface relating to the recent volume of "Essays and Reviews." By the Rev. GEORGE MOBERLY, D.C.L., Head Master of Winchester College. Second Edition. 8vo., 10s. 6d.

MONRO.—Sermons, chiefly on the Responsibilities of the Ministerial Office. By the Rev. EDWARD MONRO, Incumbent of Harrow Weald. 8vo., cloth, 7s.

PUSEY.—Parochial Sermons, preached on various occasions. By the Rev. E. B. PUSEY, D.D. 8vo.

I. At the Consecration of Grove Church. 6d.
II. Christ the Source and Rule of Christian Love. 1s. 6d.
III. The Preaching of the Gospel a Preparation for our Lord's Coming. 1s.
IV. God is Love. Whoso receiveth one such little
V. Child in My Name, receiveth Me. Two Sermons, 1s. 6d.

VI. The Day of Judgment. 6d.
VII. Chastisements neglected, forerunners of greater. 1s.
VIII. Blasphemy against the Holy Ghost. 1s.
IX. Do all to the Lord Jesus. 6d.
X. The Danger of Riches.
XI. Seek God first, and ye shall have all. Two Sermons, 1s. 6d.

PUSEY.—Sermons preached before the University of Oxford. By the Rev. E. B. PUSEY, D.D. In one vol. 8vo., 9s.

Patience and Confidence the Strength of the Church. 1843. 1s.
The Holy Eucharist: a Comfort for the Penitent. 1843. 1s. 6d.
Entire Absolution of the Penitent. 1846. Two Sermons. 1s. 6d. and 1s.
The Rule of Faith, as maintained by the

Fathers and Church of England. 1851. 1s. 6d.
The Presence of Christ in the Holy Eucharist. 1853. 1s. 6d.
Justification. 1853. 1s.
All Faith the gift of God.—Real Faith entire. Two Sermons. 1855. 2s.

PUSEY.—Parochial Sermons. From Advent to Whitsuntide. Vol. I. Third Edition. 8vo., cloth, 10s. 6d. Vol. II. Third Edition. 8vo., cloth, 10s. 6d.

SEWELL.—A Year's Sermons to Boys. Preached in the College Chapel, Radley. By the Rev. Dr. SEWELL. Second Edition. 8vo., cloth, 7s. 6d.

The Practical Christian's Library.

AUGUSTINE.—The Confessions of St. Augustine. 18mo., cloth, 2s.

A KEMPIS.—Of the Imitation of Christ. By Thomas a Kempis. Four Books. A cheap Edition, entire. 18mo., cloth, 1s.

BONWICKE.—The Life of Mr. Ambrose Bonwicke. Second Edition. 18mo., cloth, 1s.

NELSON.—The Life of George Bull, D.D., sometime Lord Bishop of St. David's. By Robert Nelson, Esq. 18mo., cloth, 1s. 6d.

PRAYER-BOOK.—A Companion to the Prayer-book, compiled from the best sources. A new Edition. 18mo., cloth, 1s.

HEYLIN.—The Doctrine and Discipline of the English Church. Extracted from the introduction to "Cyprianus Anglicus," or the Life of Archbishop Laud. By Peter Heylin, D.D. 18mo., cloth, 8d.

HOOKER.—Of Divine Service, The Sacraments, &c. Being selections from Hooker's Fifth Book of the Ecclesiastical Polity. A new Edition. 18mo., cloth, 1s. 6d.

JONES OF NAYLAND.—Tracts on the Church; containing—An Essay on the Church, &c. By the Rev. W. Jones, of Nayland. 18mo., cloth, 1s. 6d.

———— On the Figurative Language of the Holy Scripture, and the interpretation of it from the Scripture itself. 18mo., cloth, 1s. 6d.

KEN.—A Manual of Prayers. By Bishop Ken. 18mo., cloth, 6d.

NICHOLSON.—An Exposition of the Catechism of the Church of England. By Bishop Nicholson. A new Edition. 18mo., cloth, 1s. 6d.

PASCAL.—Thoughts on Religion, translated from the French. By Blaise Pascal. A new Edition. 18mo., cloth, 1s. 6d.

SHERLOCK.—The Practical Christian, or Devout Penitent. By Dr. Sherlock. With a Life of the Author, by his former pupil, Thomas Wilson, D.D., sometime Lord Bishop of Sodor and Man. 18mo., cloth, 4s.; or in four parts, sewed, 1s. each.

SPINCKES.—The True Church-of-England-Man's Companion in the Closet; or, A complete Manual of Private Devotions, collected from the writings of eminent Divines of the Church of England. Compiled by the Rev. Mr. Spinckes. 18mo., cloth, 1s. 6d.

THEOLOGICAL AND DEVOTIONAL WORKS.

The Practical Christian's Library—continued.

SUTTON.—Learn to Live. By CHRISTOPHER SUTTON, D.D. *A new Edition.* 18mo., 1s. 6d.

———— Learn to Die. By CHRISTOPHER SUTTON, D.D. *A new Edition.* 18mo., 1s.

TAYLOR.—The Golden Grove; a choice Manual, containing what is to be believed, practised, and desired, or prayed for. By BISHOP JEREMY TAYLOR. 18mo., *cloth*, 9d.

———————— The Rule and Exercises of HOLY LIVING; in which are described the means and instruments of obtaining every virtue, and the remedies against every vice. 18mo., *cloth*, 1s. 6d.

———————— The Rule and Exercises of HOLY DYING; in which are described the means and instruments of preparing ourselves and others respectively for a blessed death, &c. 18mo., *cloth*, 1s. 6d.

The above two volumes in one, 2s. 6d.

WILSON.—A Short and Plain Instruction for the better understanding of THE LORD'S SUPPER, with the necessary preparation required. A new Edition, reprinted entire. By BISHOP WILSON. 32mo., *cloth*, 1s.

Also an Edition with Rubrics in red, *cloth*, 32mo., 2s.

———————— Sacra Privata. Private Meditations, Devotions, and Prayers. Adapted to general use. 32mo., 1s.

With red Rubrics, *cloth*, 32mo., 2s.

THE PENNY POST.—A Church of England Illustrated Magazine, issued Monthly. Price One Penny.

ENLARGEMENT OF THE PENNY POST.

With the January number of 1863 this Magazine was enlarged to Thirty-two Pages, with numerous Illustrations, containing Tales, Stories, Allegories; Notes on Religious Events of the Day; Essays, Doctrinal and Practical. The object is to combine amusement with instruction; to provide healthy and *interesting* reading adapted for the Village as well as the Town. A part of each number is devoted to the "Children's Corner." The Editor's Box will be continued.— Monthly, One Penny. Subscribers' names received by all Booksellers and Newsmen.

Vols. I., II., III., and IV., of the Old Series, crown 8vo., cloth, may be obtained, price 1s. 6d. each.

Vols. I. to VIII. of the New Series, 8vo., in handsome wrapper, 1s.; or in cloth, 1s. 8d. each.

16

CPSIA information can be obtained
at www.ICGtesting.com
Printed in the USA
BVHW041548030719
552601BV00012B/268/P

9 781164 855347